a
TREASURY
of
ALASKANA

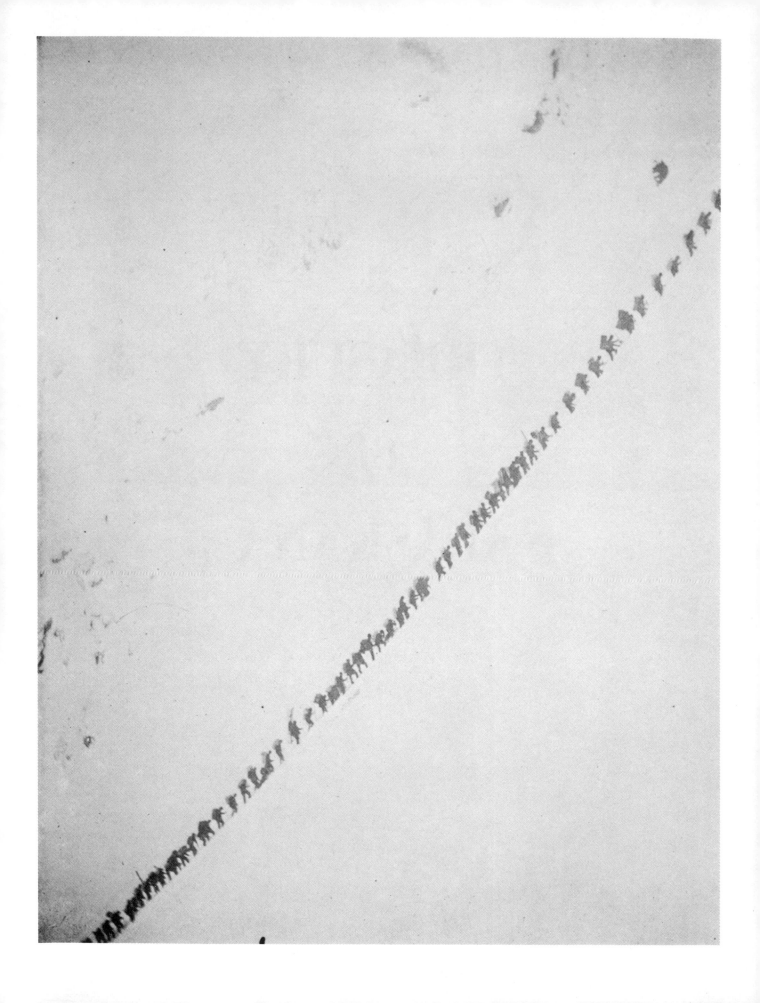

A TREASURY OF
ALASKANA
by Ethel A. BECKER

LONG, LONG TRAIL (opposite) to Chilkoot Summit, 1897 (Hegg photo).

Bonanza Books • New York

Dedication

*To the many photographers
who bequeathed to us
their undeniable
images of the past*

Foreword

This is a "picture story" of Alaska, or Aliaska as it was known in the earliest days . . . a fabulous area of 586,000 square miles . . . more than twice as big as Texas . . . one-fifth the size of the United States yet with a population comparable to a moderate-sized city in one of the older states.

Some 40,000 of its people are Aleuts, Eskimos and Indians, more than one-fifth serving in the armed forces with their dependents. And the average age of Alaskans is 26 years.

In 1958 the value of Alaska coal mined was $6½ millions, of gold $7½ millions. Prospectors still search out minerals—gold, uranium, zinc, chromite, antimony, copper, mercury, nickel, lead, silver, tin, tungsten, platinum, oil, gems, and a dozen other substances.

In Alaska over 30,000 acres of farm land are under cultivation. Only 30% of its area is covered by this agriculture and its forests. 70% constitutes mountains, mossy tundras, rivers, islands and swamps.

The commercial fish catch averages some $80 millions a year.

About one-third of Alaska lies north of the Arctic Circle where summers are hot and short and are followed by blizzardy winters.

Alaska boasts a university at Fairbanks, schools, newspapers, airlines, radio and television stations.

Alaska's income of over $500 millions a year is ever increasing, its future made more promising since its admission to the United States of America.

In this book I have tried to portray the "treasure" of Alaska's heritage in its history, people and various activities.

ETHEL A. BECKER

Contents

a
TREASURY
of
ALASKANA

BLEAK PROSPECT (opposite) Northern coastline of Siberia where Promyshleniki raided native villages and where Behring later explored (Hegg photo).

Raiders from Siberia

Alaska in the 17th century was little known land, a vast domain peopled by several nations, each divided into tribes, each tribe functioning in its own territory. Theirs was an heroic example of man's struggle to adapt himself to most extreme conditions of nature.

The Aleut nation, an estimated 8,000 souls, lived along the Aleutian Islands and Aliaska Peninsula. Their barabaras, low-slung and half-dug into the ground, were designed to withstand sub-zero storms and long dark winters. Because of the treeless prospect the Aleuts built with material at hand—driftwood, sod, skins, whalebones or perhaps fragments of canvas salvaged from the sea.

They were a short muscular people, blessed with unusual endurance so necessary to survival; a gentle and trusting people, given to laughter and games, until the invasion of fur gatherers from Siberia.

These were the Promyshleniki, daring breed of men, an inbreeding of Kurd, Cossack and bandit Chinese who began to write a bloody chapter in Aliaska's history. They had battled the Mongol tribes of Ghengis Khan and in 1636 established the far outpost of Okhotsk on the eastern edge of Siberia and then reached out for seal, sable and otter in the new land. They had two objectives—the ruthless slaughter of these animals and cruel subjugation of the natives. No longer were little villages safe.

Barabaras which would withstand the most violent storms, literally exploded under the 'thunder and lightning sticks' which the intruders turned against them. The fur wealth of the Aleutians now poured into Siberia, reviving Chinese trade. The fur tax stimulated Russia's treasury.

Trading companies which planted themselves in Aliaska were given medals by the Czar. He cancelled debts of trading merchants and their criminal crews, that they might join the Promyshleniki. Russia's expansion became the talk of Europe. The 'trading' nobility entered the despised merchant class and Russia hastened to organize trading companies which would give her priority in the discovery of the Pacific Coast of America.

11

Little girls fell victims to the Promyshleniki. It was a sad day for the natives when the white winged ships from Siberia bore down upon the Aleutians.

Fur-crazy and woman-hungry, the barbarian fur gatherers spread wide their reign of terror, rape and slaughter. Native women and girls were carted away to filthy ships to sew, cook and amuse their drunken captors, while the Aleut men roamed the tundras struggling to trap the impossible amounts of furs necessary for ransom. When women sent ashore to pick berries or fetch water escaped, hostages on shipboard were tortured and thrown overboard, their mutilated bodies instilling submission among the others. With all able-bodied Aleuts drained away to serve the invaders, famine stalked the native villages, for old men, old women and boys could not prepare sufficient amounts of food for winter.

The long-suffering Aleuts rebelled, finally. Though their weapons were no match for the 'fire sticks,' by banding themselves together, they could outnumber the enemy. Under the guise of friendship they ambushed landing parties and killed the traders. They destroyed camps and food and the sick. Full of scurvy and tortured by winter, the Promyshleniki with their fur trade and profit threatened, sought reprisal.

Ivan Solovief, the cruelest trader of them all, planned quick retaliation—either subjugation of the Aleut or complete annihilation. Cruising slowly among the islands, he fired cannon into the villages before dynamiting the barabaras and slashing survivors. He tied up Aleuts by the dozen and fired into the living target. Under such treatment, the natives became passive but never loyal.

The Siberian Eskimo was of larger stature than his Aliaskan brother. His 'mazinka' house made of walrus skins stretched taut over a whalebone framework and weighted with rocks, erupted from some volcanic peak nearby.

OLD PETER and Aleut barabara at Akutan. 100-year old native in this 1880 photo had bitter memories of rape and pillage of his people by invaders (Gabbett photo).

NATIVE VILLAGE, Naknek River, Bering Seat (Gabbett photo); below, Aleut homes in Kodiak (photo Huntington Library).

NATIVE VILLAGE, Kings Island, Bering Sea (photo Huntington Museum); below, Aleut grave poles, Kodiak (photo Huntington Library).

ATTU, Aleut village on Attu Island at end of Aleutian chain. Solovief and his men raided many such settlements, firing cannon into them from ship, then once ashore dynamiting the barabaras, slaughtering the helpless. (Gabbett photo.)

ESKIMO WOMEN prepared to carry young.

ANIMAL SKINS, fur inside, were conventional dress of Siberian Eskimos (photo Huntington Library).

ESKIMO VILLAGE (opposite) near St. Michael built of driftwood over holes dug in ground. Fish caught by women through holes in ice drying on racks. Other winter food was seal blubber, whale meat, occasional ptarmigan (photo Huntington Library).

NATIVE HOUSES (below) of Siberian Eskimos (photo Huntington Library).

SEAS WERE HOME (above) to early Eskimo people. Loathe to venture far into interior, they traveled hundreds of miles in floppy skin boats called oomiaks, skipping from one island to next (Hegg photo, 1900)

SKIN TENTS of Arctic camp in which Siberian Eskimos lived until snows came (photo Huntington Library).

ESKIMOS SUMMER HOME, shelter supplied by overturned oomiaks. River mouths were favored camping spots. Salmon spawned here and tom-cod was plentiful. Cleaned and hung on poles, catch was dried by winds and midnight sun. Prior to 18th century, Eskimos dressed in skins, ate food raw, fashioned tools and implements from stone and bone—theirs a civilization of stone age character (A. Curtis photo).

Siberian Eskimo's Mazinka House

SIBERIAN ESKIMOS were of larger stature than Aleut brothers. Mazinka houses were made of walrus skins stretched taut over whalebone framework, weighted with volcanic rocks (Roger Dudley photo, 1902)

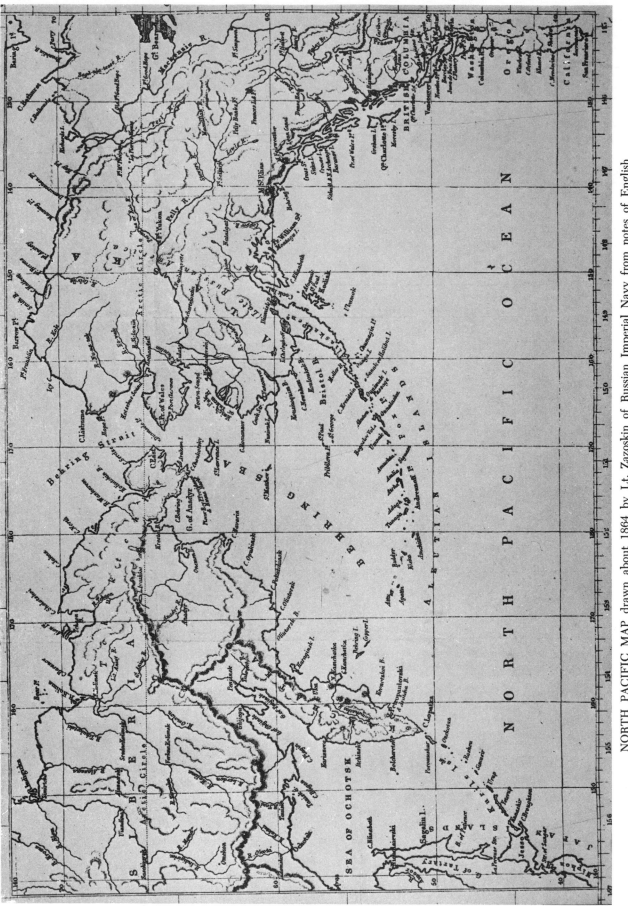

NORTH PACIFIC MAP drawn about 1864 by Lt. Zazoskin of Russian Imperial Navy from notes of English explorer F. Whymper and C. E. Arrowsmith of Western Telegraph Expedition.

ISLAND IN ERUPTION. Perry Island, center, as it appeared in 1906, 4 years after rising from Bering Sea. It sank some years later. At left is Castle Rock which appeared in 1779, at right Fire Island, showing itself in 1883 (Nowell photo from Dr. Ebert, USS *Perry*).

Russians Occupy the Land

Peter the Great, in 1720, ambitious for Imperial Russia, coveted the wealth being brought from Peru and Mexico by Spain and Portugal. England and Holland were bringing spices from the East Indies, tea and silk from China, and furs from the Antarctic. This guaranteed prosperity for the recipients; and the secret of that prosperity was in ships and an organization called the East India Trading Company whose nucleus of stockholders were adventurers, explorers and merchant seamen, all subsidized by the mother company.

Such organization, plus the colonization which followed discovery of the new land, stimulated every European treasury. Peter the Great eyed America as he studied world maps and searched out vagabond sailors. Was America joined to Siberia? No one knew. In 1723 Peter the Great organized the Archangel Whaling Company, patterned after the East India companies, and in 1728 Vitus Behring, a young Dane in the Russian Navy was sent on a secret investigation.

From St. Petersburg, Behring crossed Siberia to Kamchatka and with hewed timbers, handmade spikes and deerskin sails, built a ship. In 1732 he set sail along the coast northward into Arctic seas.

The region was barren, a place still in creation, where volcanoes belched smoke, fire and ashes. The earth trembled as an island raised a steaming head from the sea before disbelieving eyes. Yet seal rookeries and otter were everywhere and foxes scurried along the beaches, as fearless as dogs.

After five years of exploration, Behring returned to St. Petersburg with charts and glowing reports of an unclaimed region prolific in fur-bearing animals, and separated by water from Siberia. Russia immediately planned a detailed exploration.

Behring equipped a second expedition with scientists, cartographers, libraries, survey instruments and a picked crew of one hundred and fifty men. With Captain Chirikof, a very able navigator, second in command, Russia's cavalcade of experts began the tortuous trek across Siberia. In June 1741 their boats, the *St. Paul* and the *St. Peter* built of hand-hewn timbers and deerskin sails rode at anchor at Petropaulovski, Siberia.

Having made final comparison of signals and charts, Behring and Chirikof marched the crew into the little church to receive the last blessing before embarking. Calm seas and blue skies favored regular communication between the ships. Then fog and storms rolling across 6,000 miles of North Pacific separated the boats. The *St. Paul*, driven far east, lost all track of the *St. Peter*. Chirikof continued on his mission, however, to explore the land to the east. Behring searched along the Aleutians for Chirikof without success. Then he too continued on a separate exploration.

Penetrating inlets and rivers, Chirikof made charts and weather reports, explored Unalaska and the Aleutians, touched Kodiak Island, sighted Mt. Elias. At the latter point he found a different topography.

Timbered hills rose to meet snowcapped mountains and deep fjords lay in centuries-old silence. Needing water and fresh meat, Chirikof dropped anchor near the future site of Sitka and sent Mate Dementief with ten armed sailors ashore with ammunition and the empty water casks. For a few days, smoke from their fires was seen, then ceased. Lacking fresh meat and water, Chirikof's crew was succumbing to scurvy. He sent a second boat in search of the first. But timbered hills became a land of no return.

When natives in hideous masks and war paint jabbered from the shore, Chirikof gave up hope for his comrades and returned home. Disease and scurvy had depleted his crew, but recorded proof of a land worthy of colonization by his Imperial Russia, was his. In 1742 Chirikof returned to North America for a more extensive exploration.

In after years the Russians continued to search for Chirikof's missing crew, but the forests held their secret. However, the Haidas gleefully told the story around their campfires, emulating wise Chief Annahootz; how he had ambled along the beach on all fours, scratching for crab and sea life, with the Russians in hot pursuit. Finally their chief had drawn the intruders into native ambush deep in the forest.

Later the Russians were to learn they had fallen victims to the Haidas, the fiercest tribe of the Thlingit nation, a tribe who sailed like Vikings along the Pacific Coast, spreading terror as they plundered for booty and slaves.

Having lost track of Chirikof, Behring continued his exploration of Aliaska unaware that he was in an almost perpetual storm center. Weeks slipped into months. The *St. Peter*, battered by heavy seas, and wind-driven five hundred miles at a time, threatened to fall apart. Ice mantled the ship. Tackles froze. Hurricanes tore at the rotting sails.

Yet Behring continued his exploration for the Czar. Lacking fresh meat and water, scurvy prostrated the crew. Mindful of his valuable records, and fearing another winter so far from home, Behring decided to return to Siberia.

En route, bedridden himself, Behring gave orders to go ashore to recuperate. The crew of the *St. Peter* landed on a barren island and spent a winter of misery, in caves. There Vitus Behring died and was buried on the island which bears his name.

FORESTS, mountains, furs were in Behring's eye when he saw this Coast Range near Iliamna Bay, Alaska. Below, land of Behring's exploration—this area later named Dutch Harbor, Unalaska (Hegg photo).

STORM CENTER, Iliamna Bay, Alaska, where *St. Peter* was almost defeated by ice and gales (Hegg photo, 1900).

AHT NATIVE (right) of Haida tribe, part of Thlinget nation, to which Chirikof's shore crew fell victim (Whymper drawing).

TIMBERED SHORES (top opposite) near Mt. Elias where Chirikof dropped anchor, sent men ashore for water and fresh meat. They did not return. (U.S. Forest Service photo); bottom opposite, Petropaulovsky, Kamchatka, where in June, 1741, boats *St. Paul* and *St. Peter,* built of hand-hewn timbers, carrying deerskin sails, rode at anchor (Whymper painting).

BEHRING'S GRAVE (left) on small knoll with Kummandor Bay in distance. Small cross was found lying in grass, large one placed by party from Russian naval vessel in 1914 (photo Alan May).

BEHRING MEMORIAL (below). Chain and anchor are said to have come from Behring's ship, *St. Peter* (photo Alan May).

NATIVE CHURCH (above) showing memorial to Behring at side, building now used as library, social hall for dances, occasional movies (photo Alan May).

DR. HRLICKA, center, and Lt. Lazeroo, decipher inscription. Others are from U.S. Cutter *Shoshone* (photo Alan May).

Slaughter of the Innocents

For a century Siberia yielded fur tribute to Russia. Fur gatherers spread out through the fur bonanza and with each party went a tax collector for the Czar. Scarcity came in time and with the extinction of fur-bearing animals, Russian trade with China and Europe dwindled.

Without foreign trade and a navy, a nation perished. Russia had neither navy nor colonization to feed her trade.

The 18th century was a time of conquest for new land the world over, and a curious search for the Northwest Passage. Rumors pinpointed a land east of Siberia, across the North Pacific Ocean. Sailors reported the land timbered because trees had been storm-cast upon the shores of Siberia. Occasionally, the carcass of a whale or walrus held a hunting implement strange to them. Eskimos in Siberia said this land across the North Pacific was endless and rich in furs, for their relatives, the Aleuts in Aliaska, had told them so.

Behring's crew, depleted by half, trapped fresh meat and gradually recuperated. Hundreds of foxes, bold with hunger, mooched about the camp.

By Spring the men had faithfully made further investigations for their Czar, and had gathered a goodly supply of furs. They built a forty-foot boat from parts salvaged from the wrecked *St. Peter,* and sailed jubilantly home with their precious data and a cargo of otter, fox and seal furs worth $50,000.

Thus, while Dutch and English immigrants were building permanent settlements in America along the Atlantic seaboard; while English and French trappers were fighting for priority in eastern Canada and along the Mississippi Valley; while the Spanish were establishing themselves in Mexico, Behring and Chirikof had been naming headlands, islands and seas, and making charts and maps from Sitka (to be)

29

POLAR BEARS in Arctic (Roger Dudley photo)

to Behring Island in the North Pacific, laying claim to new territory for Russia which permanent settlements would later reinforce.

Arrival of the new *St. Peter* at Petropaulovski with its cargo of otter, fox and seal skins, aroused the fur traders of all Siberia in 1742. Independent trading companies sprang up everywhere, seeking boats and fur gatherers to sail to America. Maps were not yet available.

Without navigators and regional charts, in ships too frail for Arctic storms, captained by inexperienced pilots, their boats were wrecked on reefs. Crews were drowned, cargos lost. Yet in three years' time when ships began to return with fur fortunes of $100,000 and more, routes between Kamchatka and Aliaska became bustling sea lanes.

The Tibendoff Trading Company of Siberia pyramided to wealthy importance through the efforts of its able navigator, Pribiloff, who searched continually for new sealing grounds. Pribiloff discovered the great rockeries quite by accident.

Fogbound, his ship drifted into shallow water. Through the fog roared the bellowing seals at mating time. The lifting denseness revealed thousands of fur seal slithering along the beaches of low-lying islands, which he called the Pribiloffs. Their catch—40,000 seal, 2,000 otter, and 15,000 pounds of walrus ivory—sent a "Glory Hallelulah!" bursting over the Russian throne.

FUR SEALS in Arctic (Robinson photo).

ALASKAN WILD FOX (Robinson photo).

IDLE BULLS at Gorbatch Rookery, Alaska. (Scheffen photo). Below, fur seal herd (Curtis and Miller photo).

BULL SEAL with harem, St. George Island (U.S. Govt. photo, Fur Seal Res. St. George Isl).

1784 Saw Seal Herds All But Annihilated

Fur traders, now feeling financially secure, did not care to endure the hardships involved. Capt. Cook's naval records were published in English with English names recorded on his maps, thereby helping to establish England's claim to his discoveries. Learning this, to counteract it, Empress Catherine of Russia, through Gov. Yakoby of Irutash, had Shelekov plant the Emperial Emblem wherever an English ship had made a rich haul. Also, in 1787 fourteen predated iron tablets inscribed "Land Under Russian Dominion" were secretly buried by Shelekov along the Pacific Coast from the Aleutians to Southern California in an attempt to establish priority.

Further, Empress Catherine informed European maritime that specific territories in the North Pacific belonged to Russia. Not one ship left Siberia for the Aleutians in 1784. Seal herds had been almost annihilated.

I Am a Walrus

The walrus, or sea cow as the natives called the walrus, was a cumbersome fellow weighing as much as 2,200 pounds in his adult twelve-foot length.

To the Eskimos he was valued for the food he furnished, his skins for shelters and for oomiaks, and his ivory tusks, sometimes six feet in length, for carvings. To the Russians these ivory tusks meant thousands of rubles in the Chinese markets.

To the walrus, the tusks were important in fierce battles he fought, and indispensable when he set his table with mollusks pried from the bottom of the sea.

His bristling muzzle, which scooped the delicacies into his mouth, was better than a spatula. He's a mangy old rascal, isn't he?

SEA OTTER, Amchitka Island (Lay photo, U.S. Fish & Wildlife)

Old Man of the Sea

Natives called the otter, with his round head and hair as gray as an old man's beard, the 'old man of the sea.' Large brown eyes wide set, looked out from a broad face. Bristling whiskers lent an expression half human, and half ruthless, at least as the Promyshleniki who hunted him.

The soft dark pelt and silvery underfur was especially favored by the mandarins of China, and royalty of Europe. A pelt might measure six feet long and bring $1600 per single skin.

The Aleuts were masters in killing otters and processing furs but historically refused to cooperate unless forced to. In order to enslave them Russians killed and scattered a great part of the Aleut nation. To ensure obedience they held two hundred daughters of the chiefs as hostage.

WHALER *ORCA* at Point Barrow, Alaska. Below, *Pacific Queen*, formerly *Star of Alaska*.

Aliaska Under Military Rule

Furs had lost their first importance by the second half of the 18th Century. Aliaska was to become only a base for further expansion; the fur trade a camouflage for that base. Catherine II was well aware that possession of American colonies could involve Russia in a struggle with other great powers also interested, especially England.

A permanent settlement now became necessary. Shelekov chose the Three Saints Bay on Kodiak Island for the first permanent colony of the Russian-American Fur Company in 1783. Alexander Baranov, a capable Siberian trader, recognized for his ability in organizing, accounting and bookkeeping—and for his ability to deal with the Aleuts—was sent as resident manager.

Three Saints Bay, curved like a horseshoe with water deep enough for vessels and a shore shelving enough to allow beaching of boats in winter. The hills devoid of timber made the settlement safe from surprise attack from natives. And the surrounding country abounded in fur-bearing animals.

Peaceful overtures to the natives of Three Saints Bay by the Russians in 1784 were met with the usual shower of arrows and spears. The past cruelty of the Promyshleniki was not so easily forgotten. When the Russians landed the natives made a night attack on the camp and a desperate nocturnal battle followed. In retaliation Shelekov discharged cannon loaded with buckshot into the native huts. Casualties were heavy.

Simultaneously with the booming sounds, the noonday sun disappeared and darkness fell. The natives frightened at the strange happening stampeded, fled to the woods, or jumped over the cliff. Captured, the Russians forced them to deliver their children, as hostages to be educated by the Russians. Shelekov, an astronomer, had chosen the time of the sun's eclipse for his attack.

Colonizing Three Saints Bay did not end the hostilities, however, until two hundred young women were added to the hostages. Shelekov's triumphant letter to Empress Catherine said "50,000 obedient subjects have been added to your kingdom."

Having established Three Saints Bay in 1784, Baranov began building a more permanent colony at Kodiak. The plans for building Russian colonies in the North Pacific, made by Shelekov and the Governor-General at Irkutsk, were far-reaching. The cities were to be dignified from the beginning, to impress foreign ships with the stability and permanency of Russian Settlements.

Eventually the story of broad tree-lined streets, well-built homes, beautiful churches and government buildings would be carried to the far corners of the earth. Obelisks in the town square honoring Russian patriarchs would link the colony with the mother country. The city would be walled, the strong gates bolted and opened only under guard in military uniform.

Each fort would have cannon pointed in all directions. The roll of drums should accompany the morning flag raising. Systematized shipping would ensure supplies and impress foreign flags. Thus would Russia extend her empire to the new land.

While carpenters built forts and living quarters, Baranov organized his fur hunters for immediate action. The preceding fifty years had made great numbers of Aleuts and Eskimos submissive, many even loyal to their Russian masters. Intermarriage was building a new race which was leaving behind the stone age status of their ancestors.

Baranov now supplied natives on Kodiak Island with modern hunting tools, seaworthy kayaks and waterproof shirts. He placed them under surveillance of second generation Aleuts made loyal through the years, whom he brought from the Aleutians. Rules to perpetuate the colony were put in order.

All native males under fifty years of age and over eighteen were subject to hunting every other year. Fur hunting locations rotated so that the fur take occurred every second year. Holding of hostages remained a 'must' though some effort was made to gain the goodwill of the Thlinget tribe, that they might up their best furs, held secretly for foreign ships bearing more desirable trade goods.

WHALER *J. H. HOWLAND* (photo Huntington Library).

Prosperity Visits Aliaska

European explorers roaming the North Pacific through the 18th Century caused untold anxiety in Russia because for the time being Russia's war with Sweden (1787) and Turkey (1788) retarded Imperial expansion and colonization. To save herself Russia encouraged her nobility to enter the merchant class and form trading companies. Prison doors were opened, releasing debtors and criminals of all kinds to join the migration of traders, sailors, ship builders, fur dealers and adventurers trekking toward eastern Siberia and eventually Aliaska.

Prosperity came to Siberian cities—Okhotsk, Petropavlovski and Plover Bay. Stores, shipyards, churches and schools were built. Trading companies stocked trade goods—needles, iron tools, cloth, tea, coffee, sugar, tobacco and kettles—more desired by the natives than furs which came from their back yard. Siberian merchants, hopeful of big fur profits, sponsored fur gathering expeditions manned by Russia's ruffians. Barter failing, they used force. The beaches grew bloody with slaughter. The natives succumbed to brutality.

ORIGINAL RUSSIAN BUILDINGS (right) at Kodiak (photo Huntington Library); below, Three Saints Bay.

HARPOONING young finback whale in Queen Charlotte Straits. Below, tying up finback (photos Dr. Gilmore, U.S. Fish & Wildlife Service).

Gregorii Ivanovich Shelekov

By 1787 Gregorii Shelekov of Rylsk, Siberia had become the wealthiest merchant in the North Pacific. Financed by a smelting works in the Ural Mountains, he held interest in fourteen of the thirty-six ships which made expeditions to the Aleutians between 1777 and 1797, and was joint owner with Golikov in other expeditions returning annually with 300,000 rubles and more in fur pelts.

Competition, already keen between Russian and Siberian trading companies, was further complicated by the appearance in the North Pacific of foreign ships, whalers and vagabond brigs loaded with sugar, glass beads, knives, tools, calico, blankets and all manner of gee-gaws dear to the native heart.

In 1776 England lost her American colonies through the Revolutionary War, and Hudson's Bay Company, under English charter, began to expertly push forts across Canada towards the Pacific Coast, building up a fur trade and colonizing as she went. And Russia, fearing for her new American discovery, began to cultivate the friendship of a weak sister, the new United States of America.

GREGORII IVANOVICH SHELEKOV (photo Juneau Museum).

ALEUT WOMAN and child in Russian dress (Hegg photo).

41

RUSSIAN PRIESTS (top row left) brought to Aliaska by Nathalie Shelekov to teach "heathens" (photo Huntington Library); center, Eskimos in wind-proof clothing (Hegg photo); right, trader with native wife and family.

ALEXANDER BARANOV, left.
(photo Juneau Museum).

ALEUT BERRY PICKER (below). Missionary schools and new way of life such as marriage with Russian, Scandinavian, French, English traders, brought many improvements among Aleuts (Nowell-Dudly photo).

RUSSIAN OVERSEER (opposite) and Aleuts (photo Huntington Library).

Cruelty with Salvation

Gregorii Shelekov owed much of his success to his wife, Natalie, the first white woman settler in Aliaska. Endowed with pioneer vision, she instinctively combined the possibilities of the new land with its needs and insisted that home life must center around school and church if permanency of the colonies be assured.

Count Zubor, related to Natalie and a favorite of Empress Catherine, made a valuable ally. Zubor impressed upon the Empress the importance of saving the heathens' souls, "so eager now to become Christians." They beseiged the synod at St. Petersburg Russia to send priests at the expense of the Russian-American Fur Company to the 100,000 natives waiting for God's enlightenment.

Hundreds of missionaries prepared to migrate to Aliaska. Shelekov built a monastery at Kodiak —"so build that the monks were unable to see what the lay brothers were doing, and vice versa." Each church became a foundation stone in Russia's Empire to the north.

Churches built by the Russians in the 18th Century still stand, a symbol to the natives of Divine guidance and power. An ikon hung in every home. Religion became a part of daily living. No hunting trip was ever started without blessings from the priest. No service went unattended. Promyshleniki sought expiation for sins at the confessional even while further cruelties were being planned.

The Russians built a church in every fur-gathering station and hung a bell in every belfry. The hearts of the natives thrilled to the muscial tones reaching into every home, every cove and inlet, instilling a certain wonder about the white man's God.

What had happened to the great White Spirit who had watched over them for as long as they could remember? Was this new God better? Their children now attended the school beside the church and were cold and hungry no more. Yet their masters were cruel. What manner of religion was this that could be cruel and kind at the same time?

GREEK ORTHODOX CHURCH (top row left) Kodiak (Hegg photo, 1900); center, interior Unalaska church (Curtis & Miller photo, 1902); right, Russian Church at Unalaska (Curtis & Miller photo, 1902).

Interior of Unalaska church reflected exquisite beauty of Old World churches. Priceless paintings by old masters adorned walls. 12 icons ornamented 3 sanctuaries. Books bound in crimson velvet graced library. Communion cup held by priest glistened in pure gold. Pearls, rubies, emeralds, diamonds sparkled in mitre. Congregation stood up in long unintelligible service.

GREEK CHURCH at Nulatto (2 views below), unpainted, crudely built but displaying delicate laces and altar cloths brought from Europe. Every native village had church where all teaching began. Shelekov curried native goodwill while holding people in cruel check. Bad priests came with good. In one village every woman and girl became pregnant while able-bodied men were away hunting (Curtis & Miller photo, 1902).

Valley of 10,000 Smokes

The Russians might subdue the natives but Mother Nature warned of a Power greater than the Promyshleniki boot. Hardly had Kodiak been established than a trembling earth sent tidal waves across the islands; destroying settlements, oomiaks, barabaras. Walrus, whale, fish and seal, bellied up, floated on a boiling tide. Natives cowered, not knowing when to flee or where.

Promyshleniki fell to their knees before the ikons. Rumbling and quaking continued for days. Then, one hundred miles from Dutch Harbor, Old Bogoslof rose from the waves (1796), spewing forth volcanic ash and smoke. The flaming cauldron dyed the clouds a bloody red, the sky and the sea. Death stalked the islands.

But no sooner had the volcanic mass cooled than mura nested in the crags and old men climbed the jagged cliffs to gather eggs and snare the birds.

The Russians named the peak 'Bogoslof,' commemorating Joanna Bogoslof, 'Old' Bogoslof because a hundred years later 'New' Bogoslof was born.

46

VILLAGE OF KARLUK (Gabbett photo, 1880).

Karluk Was Typical Fur Station

90 miles from Kodiak, Karluk on Shelekov Straits was symbolic of fur gathering stations built within easy access of the Aleutians and the mainland.

In spawning season, the Karluk River, sixteen miles long, ten feet deep and from one hundred to six hundred feet wide, became a river of salmon which yielded 60,000 fish in a single seine. Here, between May and September, came natives from near and far to dry their winter's food supply. Here they salted barrels of fish for their Russian masters. And the church on the hilltop occupied the dominant position.

47

DRYING FISH for dog food (Gabbett photo).

BIRDS ON OLD BOGOSLOF ISLAND (Kluckholm photo). Collecting and salting furs in each settlement was supervised by Russians. Elders or Tinyons were chosen from loyal natives proficient in hunting and management. Tinyons were overseers of fur hunters, sent old men and children out hunting birds, assigned women to clean fish, pick berries, sew parkas. Each Tinyon received a fine suit of clothes decorated with buttons and gold braid. While Baranov was founding colonies along the coast and gathering furs, Shelekov was seeking new markets for Russian trade.

POLITKOFSKY—last gunboat built by Russians in Aliaska, passing into American hands when country was sold in 1867. Ship was later remodeled into tug boat for lumber mills of Puget Sound in Washington State.

Fur Company Hold Strengthened

When Shelekov died in 1795 without securing a protective fur agreement, his fur company found itself with no real hold on Aliaska. Whereupon Natalie, Shelekov's wife, donned her war bonnet, lined it with diplomacy, and headed for St. Petersburg, Russia with her son-in-law, Rezanov, in tow. After four years she got her charter but not until the headquarters of the Russian-American Fur Company had been transferred from Irkutsk, Siberia, to St. Petersburg, Russia where Natalie could use her political connections.

Natalie brought home a good charter, extending twenty years with a subsidy and exclusive rights to gather furs in Aliaska territory north of 55 degrees. This charter was renewed until 1859 and the company began building sturdy patrol boats armed for and aft with guns.

FOUR-MASTED SCHOONER (Historical Museum, Tacoma).

49

BARANOV'S ALEUT BRIGADE (sketch from *Vancouver's Voyage*).

Fighting for Fur

Baranov's explorations took him as far south as Vancouver Island. Everywhere "King George" men and "Boston" men were trading energetically for furs with the natives. Baranov chose Sitka as the strategic place for the next permanent settlement. In 1799 a fleet of five hundred bidarkas, each manned by two and three Aleuts, set out from Kodiak under convoy bound for Sitka, twelve hundred miles southeast.

Six miles from the village of the Sitkas, Baranov received a piece of tribal land from Chief Skayentelts in trade for tea, coffee, tobacco, pots and pans and a bolt of calico. There he began construction of New Archangel, the Sitka of today.

Now, just as the English government hid behind the East India Trading Company for 200 years, so did the Czarist government plot for a century mastery of the Pacific, hiding behind the name of the Russian-American Fur Company.

Legend says that sailors from the English ship *Unicorn* led the attack when the Kolosh burned Baranov's new fort in 1802, stole 2700 otter skins, and kidnapped Russian workers.

History relates that Captain Barber diplomatically—since peace had been agreed between Russia and England—commanded that Chief Skayeutelt safely return both furs and Russian prisoners to the *Unicorn*. Capt. Barber then set sail for Kodiak with the captives and demanded a ransom of 50,000 rubles' worth of furs from Baranov.

Baranov, himself adept in diplomacy, dickered the demand to 10,000 rubles' worth of furs. And the *Unicorn* sailed away loaded to the gunwales with a fortune in sea otter skins, ransomed and otherwise.

When the Czar learned of this 'outrage,' he sent Baranov a secret order: "All work in northern areas must cease until possessions adjacent to the English in the Pacific had been strengthened." (Okun)

THLINGETS IN POTLATCH DRESS. A barbaric nation, Thlingets wore rings in nostrils, painted themselves hideously. Stubborn fighters, accurate with spears, bows and arrows, they were ferocious in hand-to-hand combat. Their heads were protected in battle by wooden helmets carved like animals. Plaited wooden armor beneath heavy elkskin parkas gave excellent protection to bodies. These were the natives Baranov dealt with in establishing new city of Sitka (Hegg photo, 1900).

ALEUT WOMAN, right (Curtis photo).

51

NATIVE GRASS HUT near Sitka; below, graves of Russian seamen (Hegg photos).

GRAVES OF RUSSIAN MIDSHIPMAN AND SIX SAILORS KILLED IN BATTLE WITH KIK-SITI INDIANS IN 1804

NEW ARCHANGEL, Sitka Sound, 1805 (photo B. C. Archives).

Trouble on All Fronts

Kodiak, the first city, prospered, land was cleared, homes were built in the shadow of the trading post. But fur hunters were not farmers and agriculture failed. Bears killed the sheep and cattle bought from Indians of Puget Sound.

Yet the population of Aleuts, Eskimos and Russians increased. The place swarmed with children begotten of Aleut women. The priest baptized them all and the settlement on Kodiak Island radiated prosperity and fur wealth.

Time replaced the low-bred criminal Russian escapees with a more refined type. Natives came to appreciate their new-found comforts. A few generations had passed and the Creoles began to show the effect of the religious training instituted by Natalie Shelekov, and the mixture of racial strains—Russian, English, Yankee, Spanish and French.

While the natives generally remained hostile to the Russians, intermarriage and education brought a dubious loyalty. Legend kept alive the mistrust and misery brought by the "outside" man. Priests assured them that the church with its crosses, bells and rituals was their protection and gradually the church and its doctrines became the anchor and place of refuge.

Leaving Baranov and thirty men to construct the fort at New Archangel (Sitka), the Aleut Brigade returned to Kodiak, gathering furs on the way. Workmen spent a miserable winter in Sitka, the new location, in downpours of rain, in leaky shelters, with poor food, and surrounded by hostile Kolosh. (The Russians called all natives from Yakutat to the Columbia River "Kolosh.")

Baranov, with his military caution, held the natives in check; but the day came when business forced him to return to Kodiak. The Kolosh watched discipline grow lax, and prepared to take over. At this time, according to Tikhmenof's records, Captain Barber arrived in the Sandwich Islands on the trading ship *Unicorn* to learn that Russia was at war with England. Immediately Capt. Barber thought of Kodiak and especially the stores of Russian furs.

After the destruction of the Russian fort at New Archangel (Sitka), English and Yankee trading vessels held undisputed sway near Sitka for several years, among the coves and islands which abounded with otter, seal, mink and beaver.

In 1804 Baranov decided to return to New Archangel and this time establish his headquarters on the actual site of the Sitka tribe. One hundred and fifty ruffian Promyshleniki and five hundred Aleuts in bidarkas left Kodiak under guard of the Russian gunboat *Neva* and moved in across from the Indian village.

Baranov sought a peaceable agreement but the Kolosh refused all offers to surrender the fortress, to make peace, or to enter into any trade agreement. The Russians began the assault, but even cannon fire failed to dent the heavy log stockade. When Baranov led his men to the attack, deadly fire mowed them down.

The Thlinget nation never allowed Baranov to forget that Sitka was built on their tribal land. Once a year they sailed into Sitka Bay, 1,000 strong, supposedly to fish and gather herring-roe on the hemlock branches which they placed in the sea.

Real fear spread through the Russian city as the hostile canoe armada cruised among the near islands. Day after day the natives fished as they waited for some sign of relaxation in the fort; for word from some woman hostage that one of the guards would not pace his beat that night. But guards had been doubled, hostages were prisoners and no word came. Each year they returned to their totem-studded villages to await a more opportune time.

The crisis would pass but the Russians knew that another spring would bring another fishing fleet to loiter in Sitka's front yard. Baranov finally solved the problem by building a district of small homes with gaudy red roofs and yellow walls for the deposed tribe on their old homestead.

Their "ranche" extended along the beach where kayaks could nose into the sand just outside the door. All this was within the shadow of the fort. There were church schools for the children and trade schools for the adults.

Sitka natives accepted Russian guidance after a fashion, gradually fitting themselves into the life of the community, still following the sea they loved, and working at various trades. So the Thlinget nation settled back to fish and gather furs. Outwardly, peace of a sort reigned though the least provocation sent them whooping for their war paint.

SKELETONS near Cape Thompson, Alaska.

VILLAGE OF KASAAN (Hegg photo, 1900); below, Russian cannon that guarded Sitka from Indian attack.

VIEWS OF SITKA

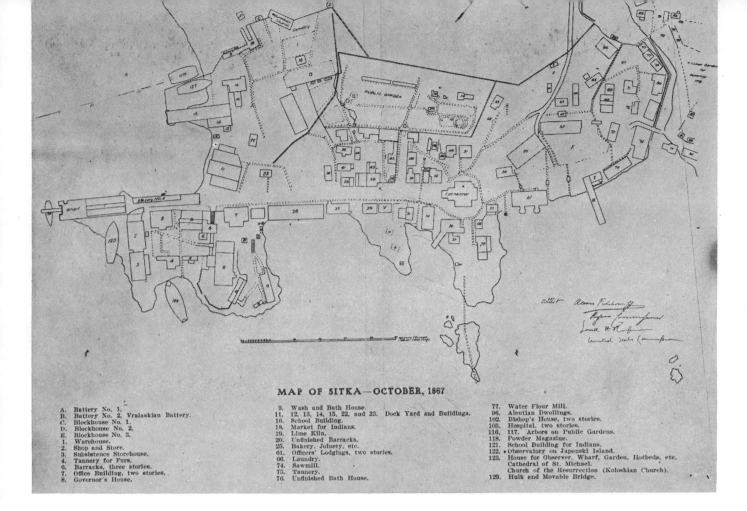

MAP OF SITKA—OCTOBER, 1867

A. Battery No. 1.
B. Battery No. 2, Vralaskian Battery.
C. Blockhouse No. 1.
D. Blockhouse No. 2.
E. Blockhouse No. 3.
1. Warehouse.
2. Shop and Store.
3. Subsistence Storehouse.
4. Tannery for Furs.
6. Barracks, three stories.
7. Office Building, two stories.
8. Governor's House.

9. Wash and Bath House.
11. 12, 13, 14, 15, 22, and 23. Dock Yard and Buildings.
16. School Building.
18. Market for Indians.
19. Lime Kiln.
20. Unfinished Barracks.
25. Bakery, Joinery, etc.
61. Officers' Lodgings, two stories.
66. Laundry.
74. Sawmill.
75. Tannery.
76. Unfinished Bath House.

77. Water Flour Mill.
96. Aleutian Dwellings.
102. Bishop's House, two stories.
103. Hospital, two stories.
116. 117. Arbors on Public Gardens.
118. Powder Magazine.
121. School Building for Indians.
122. Observatory on Japonski Island.
123. House for Observer, Wharf, Garden, Hotbeds, etc.
      Cathedral of St. Michael.
      Church of the Resurrection (Koloshian Church).
129. Hulk and Movable Bridge.

Sitka—City of Hope

Plans for development of Sitka were elaborate but building a city in enemy territory far from the source of supply was no sinecure, even for a man of Baranov's ability. Sitka was to know many periods of near-starvation because all supplies must be brought in. Furs must be gathered and shipped away to defray expenses and Russian cruelty to the Kolosh did not stimulate either friendship or cooperation.

Every activity had to be performed under guard. Women hostages wangled secrets from their masters even as they bedded with them. Snapping black eyes lured guards from their stations. Pelts were stolen. Guns and ammunition disappeared. And while every Russian project was being sabotaged, English and American vessels sailed boldly in and out bearing away a king's ransom in furs.

Baranov schemed for every fur he took. Lacking hunters he now raided far-away Japan and placed Japanese prisoners on his island of Japonski until he could train them to hunt with the Aleuts. He planned intermarriage with Indian princesses. He himself married the daughter of a chief. Little by little the barriers crumbled, and Sitka began to fulfill her destiny as the Queen City of the North Pacific.

Block houses were erected in Sitka in strategic locations and soldiers were on constant duty. Guns were always loaded and musket barrels gleamed through the aperatures. Through the night sentries signalled from post to post. Strictest military discipline prevailed at all times, for sooner or later the natives would mass to burn and slaughter the lot of them.

As Sitka was being guarded and built, Aleut fur hunters far from home must be guarded to be sure the take of furs might increase and so make the Russian project goodly in the sight of the Czar.

Baranov's castle stood on a bluff overlooking the city, a hundred feet above the sea. Barracks, storehouses and other buildings were surrounded by sturdy log palisades cut from trees which grew within easy reach of a windlass. Solid log towers commanded a good view of enemy approach.

BARANOV ISLAND, now part of Tongass National Forest (U.S. Forest Service photo).

Land of Waste and Want

With its secluded lakes and streams, Baranov Island afforded excellent hunting. Flotillas of bidarkas under convoy moved into far inlets trapping or gathering furs already taken by the natives. The Gulf of Kenai in the beginning yielded 3,000 skins and more per year. Fifty bidarkas collected 750 to 1000 otter a season. Ten years later otter had almost disappeared and one hundred skins only were taken. To overcome the loss, Baranov granted contracts to ships trading beyond the Russian American possessions and increased the otter-take to 8,000 skins between 1808 and 1812.

There was much careless waste. Skins rotted because of improper curing. Full storehouses had few saleable skins. In the Aleutians 30,000 seals were killed for the flesh alone. As profits to the shareholders of the Russian American Fur Company decreased, Baranov cast his eyes on virgin territory, far north and far south.

Starvation threatened at all times for able-bodied men were being sent out fur gathering when they should have been fishing for winter. Old men, women and children were not able to store food enough for the tribe, and when they did, the Russians robbed them to replenish their own slim cupboard.

ANCIENT GREEK CHURCH, Sitka (right)—photo Britten & Rey; below, Russian priest in ceremonial robe (photo Newell & Dudley, 1904).

Priests Had the Power

Not until 1833 when Etholin became the governor did the church school become very efficient, when pupils were trained to work for the company. Courses included religious training, reading, writing, grammar, mathematics, astronomy, bookkeeping and navigation. The best pupils were sent to St. Petersburg, Russia, for advanced training. Church trade schools also trained pilots, clerks, cooks, bakers, surveyors, mapsmen, engravers, ship masters and such.

In 1842 a beautiful church replaced an earlier Greek Orthodox structure. The church was given a 'dry' share in every venture of the fur company —a 'dry' share requiring no payment. Thus, and by naming colonies and islands after the saints, they hoped for blessings for themselves.

The church was closely associated with the government in that the charter demanded that the church and priests who came from monasteries in Russia be well cared for. However, there was much friction between priest and fur hunter.

One duty of the priest was to perform rituals to speed the departing hunters. The hunting brigade, often numbering 1,000 kayaks, set out for the mainland in April and returned in August.

On leaving Sitka the kayaks were drawn up in a row, prow resting on the sand, hunting paraphernalia tied to the deck, each hunter standing silent beside his kayak as the priest came solemnly from the church. His choristers chanted a blessing as each hunter was sprinkled with holy water. The hunters crossed themselves, and as they pushed off and headed out to sea with a gunboat escort, a cannon salute from the fort wished them God-speed.

Theirs was a dangerous mission in enemy territory where treacherous natives always lay in wait. The escort picked up furs as they were gathered. In early fall they returned home to a time of feasting and blessing.

Plenty of Skins—Little Grain

Sitka knew hunger, due to frequent shortage of grains to be ground into flour and meal. One food crisis was alleviated in 1806 when the *Juno*, 850-ton American sailing ship, arrived with grain, butter, sugar and molasses.

Baranov bought the vessel and its entire cargo. Reloading the ship with furs, beads, knives, linens, calicoes and ribbons, he sent Resanov to California to seek a trade agreement for dairy products and grains. Though the *Juno's* cargo was highly desired, officials at Bogeda Bay, California held out against any exchange, for Spanish law forbade foreign trading in California.

The Franciscan Fathers of California, ever thankful for the copper bells which had come from Sitka's foundries, eyed their own bulging grain bins regretfully. Now the Spanish governor had a bosom friend and the bosom friend had a well-bosomed, black-eyed daughter, Conception Arguela, who desired very much the linens and pretties tucked away in the *Juno's* cargo. For a few days she was a busy little lady and soon every woman there desired the pretties stored aboard the ship. "How foolish to return goods so badly needed," reasoned the menfolk. The romance between Resanov and Conception of California is one of the great love stories of history— all of which led to a trade agreement between Russia's Resanov and the Spanish governor.

Baranov's castle looked down on a harbor whose hustle would have done credit to any third-rate port in the civilized world. The beacon which burned in the turret never failed to direct mariners through the maze of islands to safe anchor.

In the fur warehouse fifteen hundred pegs stuck into the rafters held fifteen hundred otter skins, valued at up to six hundred dollars per

skin. Thousands of furs hung against the walls and from beams in the underground cellars— sable, martin, weasel, beaver, fox (silver-grey, blue, white, red and black), ermine, muskrat and seal. Thousands of skins lay baled in rectangular blocks, bear skins, wolf skins and tons of ivory from northern walrus herds.

And woe to any Aleut or Russian who traded furs to English or Yankee ship masters for coveted blankets and guns. Arrest and deportation to Siberia were a certainty.

GRINDSTONES FOR FLOUR MILLING (Hegg photo, 1900).

NATIVES AND TRADERS at St. Michaels (photo Huntington Library).

INDIAN VILLAGE (below) near Hazleton, B.C. "Devil chasers" were placed on some graves.

TOTEM POLE on Skeena River (Curtis photo); below, Russian warehouses, Stika.

TOTEM POLES at Prince Rupert (Curtis photo).

BIRD TOTEM POLE (below) on Skeena River (Curtis photo).

WHALER *BELVIDERE*

Trading with the World

Hundreds of sailing vessels came to the North Pacific in search of furs. Whaling vessels gloried in the abundant schools of whales. Natives, while saving a few furs for the Russians, saved the best for the arrival of foreign ships—the English, Spanish, and Americans. Many flew no flag as they scooted in and out.

Salmon from the freezing waters of the North Pacific became a favored commodity far and wide around the world. Great schools of the fish, returning north to spawn still choked the far rivers of Aliaska every year.

With the increased demand for salted salmon in Tahiti and the Hawaiian Islands, the Russians built salting houses in their fur-gathering stations. Hundreds of barrels of salmon bellies were prepared for shipment. Only the belly of the salmon was salted, because of its flavor and fat content.

Ships from around the world berthed at Naknek, Aliaska, at high tide to take on cargoes of fish. At low tide, Naknek faced a broad mud flat.

Trading posts and forts of the Russian American Fur Company were now extended along the Arctic seas and up the Kuokuk, the Kuskaquiem, along the broad Yukon and their tributaries. The natives were more friendly here, trapping, fishing and hunting in birch bark canoes. Kill they would, however, to right a wrong or to eliminate an unwanted intruder. Originating from Athabascan stock, the natives had migrated from the east, and eked out a precarious living drying berries, fish and caribou meat.

Penetrating into interior Aliaska, the Russians turned the native villages into trading posts and forts. St. Michael, Anvik, Nulatto and Fort Yukon held a mixed crowd of Siberians, Finlanders, Aleuts, Creoles, Eskimos and pure Russians, the

64

latter supervising the natives and trading for furs. The belligerent Tananas who roamed the country between the Tanana and the Yukon River forbade trespass. In time, however, they came curiously to Fort Yukon, in holiday dress, in skins, painted faces and heads dabbed with red clay from which protruded small feathers. Colored beads they loved and stored away. For guns, blankets, knives and pots they gave their choicest furs.

Natives in their villages at the mouth of the rivers caught fish to dry. They killed bear, caribou, moose and other fur-bearing animals but there were many lean months. Placing trade goods before the village on a slab of bark or bit of lumber on an incoming tide, the boatmen waited for a return of fur goods. Thus did trading take place.

NAKNEK RIVER (top), Bering Sea (Kluckholm photo, 1890); (bottom) trading ship laying to for native furs (Dudley photo).

ANVIK on Yukon River, ducks and ptarmigan curing on racks (Hegg photo, 1900); Below, sea otter, floating near Amchika Island with paws on chest. With fresh source of fur supply found in south sea otters became plentiful. Unmindful that Aleuts and hunters were closing in, playful sea otter would float on back for hours (Jones Jr. photo U.S. Fish & Wildlife Service).

BARANOV'S CASTLE, 1887.

Baranov Dies at Sea

By mid-century Sitka was world-famous. Every seaman's desire was to visit Sitka once before he died, to meet the man Baranov who had wrought such wonders in libraries, schools, industries and shipyards, to attend a gay party in the castle on the hill. Guests who had hobnobbed with royalty were amazed at the ornate furniture, rich decorations, priceless paintings and a library with books written in every language.

Banquets were lavish indeed, worthy of the powerful corporation whose domain was greater than most kingdoms, and whose influence was building an empire in the north. Priests attended, and bishops dignified in brocaded robes; military men in gold-braided uniforms, officers of foreign ships, and secretaries, storekeepers, accountants. Indian chiefs and wives of high Russians added flavor.

But Baranov was growing weary. Twenty years had seen every marker placed by Shelekov, replaced with a fort or settlement. Natives had been subdued. Now old and rheumatic, Baranov asked to be relieved. In 1818 the Czar sent a successor, a military man and Baranov sailed for home, to pass away en route and be buried at sea.

Military governors followed Baranov's death, each serving a four-year term. The British had begun to distrust the Americans, moving west, settling as they went. The Russians feared the British and kept a wary eye on the Americans whom they favored above the British. The American found the west a great land with room for everyone, while the native prayed they would all go home and allow him to settle back in peace in his old hunting ground.

Rivalry between British and Russian traders reached a climax in 1825. The Hudson's Bay Company sent Mr. Pelly, its governor and Sir George Simpson, governor of Rupert's Land, to St. Petersburg, Russia, to establish boundary lines against Russian advancement. In the peaceful agreement forthcoming, latitude 54-40 became the boundary line between English and Russian territories, with the Russian northwest boundary in no case to be extended beyond ten marine leagues from the sea.

It also granted the English free navigation of streams flowing from Canadian territory across Russian land. This referred particularly to the Stikine River. To protect Russian fur trade, the Russians extended forts in places strategic for barter with the natives.

FATHER DUNCAN in his study (Hegg photo).

Father Duncan Comes to Metlak-Atla

Various church denominations considered the north ripe for missionary work. In 1857 Father Duncan, a young English layman, came to Fort Simpson, the most important Hudson's Bay trading post on the Pacific Coast.

The savage Tsimshian nation, numbering some 14,000, practiced cannibalism and slavery. They had the wildest orgies. Paradoxically, they were a talented people, skilled in carving in wood, stone and ivory.

It was not an easy assignment Father Duncan chose. Gaining the loyalty and cooperation of some sixty natives, Father Duncan began to clear land, erect a school house, stores, canneries and a mill, all organized on a cooperative plan. In his quiet manner he taught the natives to build homes, tan leather and make shoes, and to build boats with white sails. A native band played for their potlatches.

Church services were very simple for no native could understand the "why" of communion and ritual. After thirty years' progress and good living

the Church of England sent a bishop to oversee Father Duncan's work, a tactical error of great proportion.

The new bishop, in his failure to understand the natives and their way of life, created friction and dissatisfaction in the community. Father Duncan watched the morale of the natives lapse, and thirty years of hard work disintegrate.

Negotiating secretly for Annette Island which lay in American territory, he moved his faithful followers and there began a new church. The new Metlakatla became self-supporting, governed by a native council, president and police force. The land belong to the community, and no white was ever allowed to be a part of its enterprise or prosperity.

In 1895 natives gazed proudly at a new church, built with lumber sawed frow their own trees, in their own mill, and fashioned with their own hands. This model of education still stands, an example of rehabilitation and a monument to Father Duncan and his people.

VICTORIA in 1858 (photo Prov. Archives, B.C.)

Threats Come from the South

Natural resources of Aliaska had begun to attract wide attention. Trappers eyed the fur trade. Fishermen calculated the products of the sea, as yet barely touched. Prospectors followed the rumors of mineral wealth.

Great cod banks had been discovered quite by accident in 1857 when the brig *Timandra* was ice-locked and the crew while fishing discovered great banks of cod. In 1865 they returned to fish commercially. Salmon they knew about—they swept up the coast in a stream a mile wide and miles long at spawning time—rivers choked on salmon en route to gravel beds on the upper lakes and streams.

Ten tons a day was an average salmon haul from fish traps already built. Salted fish found a constant market. California now canning its fish found the product superior and eyed the Arctic supply greedily, concerned over fishing in Russian-claimed waters. That was the salmon story. What about the cod banks they had found? Fish wealth was no longer a secret.

Since 1835 difficult times had been in store for the Russian-American Fur Company. Markets were insecure and hard to get because England had found new methods of processing furs. The treasury was low. The eternal food problem had never been permanently solved.

Discovery of gold in California in 1848 brought a flood of immigrants who needed all the grain and food California could raise, which curtailed food shipments to Sitka. Immigrants overflowed northward, settling as they came. New towns sprang up along the Pacific Coast—Olympia, Seattle, Port Townsend, Victoria, Tacoma and Portland.

Forest products competed with furs. Handmade 'shakes' (shingles) replaced furs as 'legal tender' from California to the Hawaiian Islands. Settlers moved into the lowlands of the northwest where grew immense cedars so necessary for making 'shakes.'

When shipping slumped, Dr. Tolmie, the Factor at Fort Nisqually continued to trade the necessities of life for 'shakes.' Dr. Tolmie hit the jackpot when gold was discovered at Sutters Creek. San Francisco became a place of tents. California had gold and settlers, but no shingles. And Fort Nisqually had a fortune in cedar shakes.

Discovery of gold in the Cariboo region of British Columbia in 1858 also had its influence on Russia's policy in Aliaska. Thousands of stampeders, disappointed at Sutter's Creek, California, swarmed into Victoria and the old Hudson's Bay trading post on Vancouver Island, to be outfitted. Every schooner and derelict of the sea was loaded to the gunwales with men and freight. Pack trains and covered wagons lurched through Oregon territory, headed for Sumas, Washington and Mission, B.C. Many dropped out along the way to settle along the fertile river valleys. Others hurried up the Fraser River and into the Cariboo gold fields, spreading into virgin land of western Canada.

Immigrants followed, to trap furs, fish, farm, homestead and raise cattle. The Russian-American Fur Company watched these rugged pioneers come and settle happily, wondering how close this threat would come to them.

Now Peter Ogden, chief trader for the Hudson's Bay Company, planned forts for the Stikine

River. Journeying to Fort Vancouver in the British brig *Dryad* he brought back cattle, trade goods, ammunition and men.

Russian gunfire from a Russian fort stopped the *Dryad* as she came up the straits, and forbade them to enter the Stikine. Ogden quoted the Treaty of 1825. The Russian answer was firm, "Stay out of the river."

Ogden returned to Fort Vancouver with the news, and Dr. McLaughlin the factor, relayed the story to London. The British fur company sued the Russian government for 135,000 silver rubles. The case hung fire until 1839, when Hudson's Bay Company was granted a lease on adjacent Russian territory, for the price of 2,000 otter skins per annum.

"Russia granted the lease, firstly, to avoid trouble with England while negotiations were under way in Europe concerning government in the straits; secondly, the lease put a limit on claims being made by the Yankees." (Okun.)

HAIDA POTLATCH DANCERS (Hegg photo, 1900); below, Teller, Alaska, showing spit.

CABLE SURVEY PARTY (above and below) at Koserefski (Hegg photos).

TELLER WATERFRONT (Hegg photo, 1900).

Cable Comes Through the Wilderness

As international business increased, speedier communication was sought between Europe and America. There were those who now remembered Behring's report of ten fathoms of water on a shallow sandy bottom in the Behring Sea between Siberia and Aliaska at Teller, Aliaska.

In 1862 Peter M. Collins, a United States commercial agent, proposed to Hiram Sibley, president of Western Union Telegraph Company, the building of a telegraph line between Aliaska and Siberia. Sibley advanced Collins $100,000 to which the United States government added $50,000 with the promise of a subsidy in 1864, and the work began.

Collins obtained the necessary charter and a right-of-way from British and Russian governments. The line was to run through British Columbia to Grantley Harbor in Aliaska, cross the Bering Straits to Siberia and connect with the Russian line, which led to Paris, London, and all Europe. The project was begun simultaneously in the Yukon Territory, Siberia and British Columbia.

Meanwhile, the Atlantic cable being laid across the Atlantic in 1865 had broken three times. Work speeded up on the Collins line and by June it connected San Francisco to New Westminster, Canada; and Colonel Buckley, on leave of absence from the U.S. Army, mapped a route through the north country.

The survey party recruited by Capt. Healy in Dawson included J. J. Watson, Chief Engineer; Major Edelsten, dog driver and hunter; Alex McDonald, Charles Roger, Maurice Harper, Moosehide Sam and two Indians. They mushed out of Dawson in 1901.

Traveling up the White River and over the divide to the Tanana Valley they laid out town sites along the right-of-way. The winter, spent at Ladue, was rugged with the temperature 66 degrees below for thirty-two consecutive days. Capt. Healy took sick with erysipelas, a disease strange to them. The party could only experiment with remedies, but with nothing but bread and condensed milk poultices, Capt. Healy did survive.

Much work had been done on the survey and right-of-way when Russia elected its first constitutional assembly in 1908, and the 'Duma' skeptical about a tunnel beneath the sea, cancelled the agreement.

Captain Libby arrived at Teller in 1866 to build the station for anchoring the cables. Simultaneously, a tall clipper ship from New York arrived at New Westminster, British Columbia, with 1,200 miles of copper wire and thousands of green insulators, the first equipment that was to link Asia with North America.

Chinese, Indians, and whites hurried up the Fraser Canyon, clearing right-of-way, erecting telegraph poles and stringing wire throughout Canada. Five hundred foremen, hundreds of packers and laborers, hundreds of pack animals packing reels of wire, sacks of insulators and supplies struggled through the wilderness. Speed was necessary to win over the Atlantic project. In August the first message flashed from Yale, B.C. to New Westminster: "Send bottle of champagne to telegraph office."

"Atlantic cable a success," so read the first telegram to Quesnel, B.C. Certain the Atlantic cable would never hold, crews kept working on the Pacific line. When the cable did hold the American end of the Collins Overland Telegraph project was abandoned. Russia, however, extended the line from Siberia to Hong Kong, Shanghai and Nagasaki. Western Union Telegraph Company, redeemed the worthless stock with a loss of $300,000. For a little while the project focussed the eyes of the world on Aliaska.

SITKA UNDER STARS AND STRIPES (Curtis & Miller photo).

U.S. TREASURY WARRANT and Agreement for sale of Alaska (photo courtesy Hist. Museum, Olympia).

Alaska Changes Flags

To sell Aliaska was not an idea generated overnight. No longer hiding behind the Russian-American Fur Company, Russia now found her problems becoming political as well as economic. She surely desired expansion, but by annexation, not by fighting on a foreign shore.

When English, Spanish and Yankee traders continued to appear in Aliaskan waters, international complications arose. England had established herself firmly in Canada. The United States was entrenched in the south. Furbearing animals of Aliaska's north neared depletion. Coffers were empty. Wages of Russian-American Fur Company employees were hard to meet. And the more important Crimean War claimed Russia's attention. Aliaska had definitely become a liability.

Long before 1860 there had been talk of selling Aliaska to the United States whose friendship Russia desired to retain.

Congress debated the purchase of Alaska bitterly. The American press was even more opposed. The New York Tribune was caustic. "According to Seward," the

Tribune stated, "there is no place in the world like Russian-America. A pleasant climate, warm in winter, where Eskimos in summer seek protection from the Arctic's burning heat. The countryside is covered with pine trees and the coast with blooming gardens. You can also find vast fields of wheat and barley, herds of seals, polar bears, icebergs, whales—and gold veins. All comforts and all necessities of life are gathered in one place and Mr. Seward assures us we shall find the white bear lolling on a bed of roses, barley ripening on the icebergs, grass growing luxurious in fields with Eskimos going sleigh riding all over the place."

Though it seemed at times that the campaign launched by the newspapers would prevent the approval of the treaty and make the proposition an international scandal, the Senate did, by vote of 37 to 2, approve the purchase on April 18, 1867.

In promoting the sale of Alaska, Hon. W. H. Seward said, "It is potentially rich. Fur, fish and timber will make it one of the great wealth-producing regions of the world. Time will commend its purchase as a great stroke of statesmanship."

Ratification of the purchase was largely due to the efforts of Baron Edouard de Stoecke, Russian minister to the United States, and time has vindicated Mr. Seward of any criticism. Charles Sumner, U.S. Senate Committee on Foreign affairs, General Banks and Thaddeus Stevens supported the purchase, for the sum of $7,250,000, for this potential Empire of the North.

The Russian navy had been bottled up in the Mediterranean and Baltic seas during the Crimean war. When civil war broke out in the United States in 1861, the Russians ordered the fleet to sail to America, anchor in New York Harbor and San Francisco Bay, so that in the event of a European war, Russia's fleet would not be rendered impotent. Citizens of the United States gladly interpreted the timely arrival of the Russian fleet as a friendly gesture during difficult times, and for this, they said, Russia was paid $250,000 of the sale price.

According to Okun's translations, $200,000 was paid for freeing and releasing the territory from all claims, privileges and grants or possessions of the united companies corporate, Russian, or foreign.

GLACIER in new U.S. territory.

Down Comes the Double Eagle

All Sitka mourned the transfer of Aliaska. There is no sadder time than when a nation lowers its flag, to pass on rule to another power. General Davis with two hundred and fifty men, armed and in full uniform, marched solemnly from the dock to the hill where stood the Governor's mansion. Simultaneously Russian soldiers advanced to the left of the flag staff from which the Russian flag still waved. The command of General Davis then formed on the right and the color guard bearing the United States flag advanced.

As the double eagle emblem of Imperial Russia began its descent, nine-inch guns of the *Ossipee* sent echoes rolling through the mountains, re-echoing the alternate firing of Russian batteries. In its slow descent the Russian emblem tangled in the ropes and refused to be lowered. The Russian bosun releasing the flag dropped it accidentally to the bayonets of Russian soldiers standing below. An evil omen, said some. The flag of the United States was raised. Captain Pestchouroff stepped forward when salutes were completed. "General Rousseau, by authority from his Majesty, the Emperor of Russia, I transfer to the United States, the Territory of Alaska." Citizens wept bitterly for Russian rule in America was no more.

Potentates and subjects had departed. The new stars and stripes flew over the beautiful city of Sitka.

What about the Russian-American Fur Company, holding now an expired charter from Russia with whom, though separate, she had been so closely allied?

Even prior to the purchase of Alaska, the Alaska-Commercial Company of San Francisco had been investigating the north. On the completion of the transfer ceremonies H. M. Hutchinson of Hutchinson & Kohl Company proceeded to the castle and arranged with ex-Governor Waksutoff to acquire the Russian-American Company's ships and other property. Later, because of Russian objection, Waksutoff became a prosperous silent partner.

Hudson's Bay Company, the English East India Company, and the Russian-American Fur Company by 1860 were also liquidated and passed into private control.

The transfer of Alaska left a bewildered citizenry in Sitka. This Alaska was home. They loved every isle, cove and mountain. Told they

SITKA and Mt. Edgecomb under U.S. regulation (photo Photo Shop, Sitka).

were free to leave when the whaler *Alexander* arrived, they wondered where they could go. Russia? A long journey and a strange land. The majority decided to stay. Time would perhaps adjust them to the new rule.

Russian dignitaries departed, abandoning native wives and children. Familiar faces disappeared from the streets.

General Jeff C. Davis moved his staff into the Russian headquarters. American soldiers quartered in the barracks. Uncle Sam's sentries paced the beats of former Russian guards. The whaler *Alexander* sailed up the Alaska coast to close up the business of the Russian-American Fur Company.

Under General Davis, military rule was well organized but no provision had been for civil law. Chaos prevailed until citizens took it upon themselves to establish a precarious city government, elect councilmen and collect revenue.

HON. W. H. SEWARD (photo Historical Museum, Olympia).

SITKA WHARF

78

WHALER *ALEXANDER* at Cape Prince of Wales, 1903 (photo Nowell-Dudley); below, Capt. Daniels with natives of Akutan (Gabbett photo).

U.S. REVENUE CUTTER *McCULLOCH* (H. P. Smith photo).

New Law of the North

The Coast Guard now became the law of the North Pacific, answering complaints of poaching on seal rookeries, quelling native uprisings, and pelagic sealing by foreign ships.

For five years the natives wandered aimlessly, without guidance, without a master to order them to fish, collect furs, build ships, and work. Revenues declined. Schools closed. City rule passed into oblivion. Even darker days prevailed when the troops sailed away in 1877, leaving government property in the hands of a collector of customs.

Natives watched the soldiers leave and old resentments flared. "Sitka is built on tribal ground," they insisted. Only the quick arrival of the *Osprey* from Fort Victoria averted massacre of U. S. officials. Privateering was common.

The *Shenandoah* left a wreckage of destroyed vessels along an entire coastline. Swooping down on a ship she set it afire. Seeing a red sky, other ships rushed to help, only to be pilfered and also set afire. Fortunes in furs, ivory, whalebones were stolen from the captured boats. Prisoners however were sent unharmed to San Francisco. The *Shenandoah* disappeared from Arctic seas finally, but not before thirty American ships had been plundered and burned.

Officers of the U.S. Navy continued to cultivate the friendship of the natives, and in time make them realize that days of slavery were past. No more would the Aleuts hunt and fish under force. No more would their women bear children for Russian masters. No more would they be scattered from the Pribiloffs to Wrangell.

While the past century had been filled with unspeakable cruelty, a new generation of Aleuts and natives had evolved from the Russian educational system, better living conditions and an organized way of life. Missionaries had taught them English and Russian. The work had only begun.

INTERIOR OF NATIVE HOME, Wrangell (Gabbett photo).

Natives No More

Natives forgot how trade goods had completely changed living conditions, furnishing their homes with clocks, chairs, beds, warm blankets and underwear. There was no need for the whites now, for they could still barter beaver, seal and otter for copper kettles, knives and spoons, for pretty beads to decorate their potlatch clothes, and for fire water which filled their potlatches with such notorious hilarity and debauchery. And for guns.

Licentiousness, fighting and killing were a constant worry to the coast guard. How many times had the U.S. government boat *Saginaw* found it necessary to incarcerate belligerent "Saginaw Jake"? All methods failed to tame him until the crew decided he "should be an officer." Decking him out in a brigadier-general's uniform, gleaming in gold braid and adorned with a policeman's star as big as a tin plate, they released him on good behaviour.

Strutting boastfully back to his village, he became an exponent for peace. He carved a wooden eagle to guard his house. It was an all-seeing eagle, he said, with a window in his chest, and no visitor was allowed to leave without seeing 'Saginaw Jake's' eagle with a "pane" in his breast.

EMANCIPATED NATIVES (above). After Russians withdrew homes were no longer broken up or little girls made to carry household burdens; right, happy girls and husky pups; below, Russian fisherman with native wife and children.

CHIMES OF GREEK CATHOLIC CHURCH at Belkofski rang out wild greetings when fur hunters returned; below, North American Commercial Co. plant, St. Michaels (Nowell photo, 1908).

A Place Forlorn

Alaska lay a place forgotten by her new United States' masters. Lethargy lay over the coves where previously hundreds of bidarkas carried enthusiastic Russian and Aleut fur-gathers.

The civil war over, the United States was absorbed with problems more complex than any Alaska could offer. Yet there were parallel problems in the new territory too, for both had slaves which had to be assimilated into a new way of life.

Several years were to pass before outlying villages were to know that Russian rule was over. In some cases four-inch shells from some native village on shore were answered by six-inch shells from a United States cruiser.

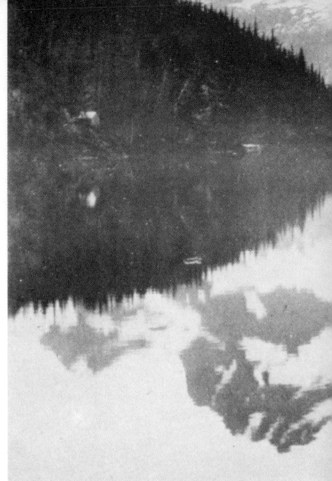

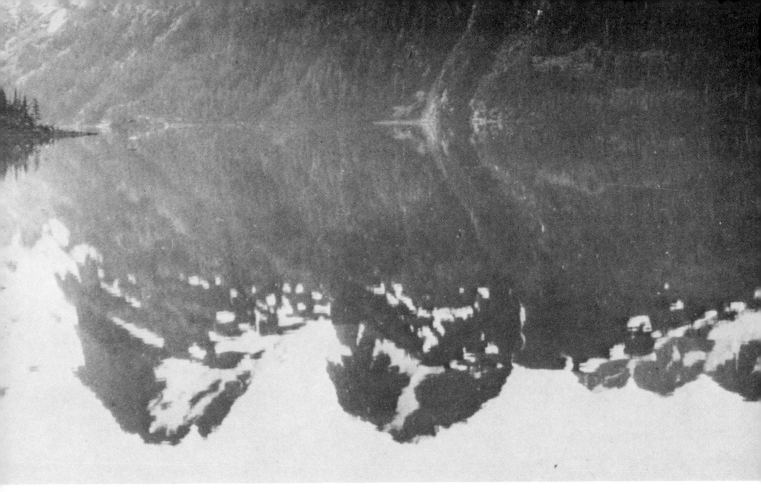

PRIBILOF ISLANDS (opposite). St. Paul and St. George Islands progressed under government control. Frame buildings replaced sod huts, native children attended grade school, some advancing education at Sitka. Priests of Russian Orthodox Church became part of Aleut lives. Islands had resident physician, dentist, oculist, hospital facilities (Curtis photo, 1900).

ALASKAN COASTAL RANGE (Hegg photo).

Forbidden Sealers on the Hunt

Sealing preserves had been thrown open by the expiration of the Russian-American Company charter. Among U.S. fur companies, Parrot & Co., Hutchinson, Kohl & Co., and Williams and Haven Co. of San Francisco were the first to land on the Pribilofs. They held off all comers, with the result that forbidden schooners began to follow the seal herd as it migrated up the Pacific Coast.

In 1894, one hundred and ten schooners took 121,143 seal skins—male, female and pups. To preserve the seal herds the United States executed a treaty with Great Britain, Japan and Russia, to discontinue pelagic sealing.

A charter embracing twenty-six years was granted the North American Commercial Company at a rental fee of $55,000 per year, plus two dollars and sixty cents for each seal and fifty-five cents for each gallon of seal oil. Annual revenue to the U.S. averaged $317,000. The North American Company also agreed to furnish natives with 25,000 dried fish, sixty cords of wood, barrels of salt for preserving seal meat, free transportation, medical and hospital care, maintain schools and care for orphans and widows. Where once the Russians gathered furs, commercial companies began to build plants for preserving fish and fur products.

KILLISNOO NATVES at Sitka potlatch (photo Case & Draper).

ALEUT CHILDREN (left) at schoolhouse in St. Paul Village and on street (below). They had much same advantages as other American children. Buildings in background are quarters for some U.S. Fish & Wildlife employees and radio station.

Flag Protected Natives' Lives

In time, natives accepted the stars and stripes as a symbol of their freedom to work and play, to attend their potlatch with its gay time of feasting and gift exchange. With flags flying the Killisnoo tribe would set out in a flotilla of high-prowed canoes to potlatch with the Sitkas.

There would be sumptuous feasts of barbecued salmon, clams, mountain goat and bear meat. There would be games, valuable gifts and dancing to the clanging copper cymbals hammered from the copper wire salvaged along the Telegraph trail.

They would dance the 'beach dance' acknowledging the Great White Spirit who fed them so bountifully from the sea and from the forest. Loaded with gifts and well fed, the visiting tribe would return home to prepare a bigger and better potlatch in the coming year, the beautiful flag of freedom flying high, binding them in a common brotherhood.

CHILKAT INDIANS, under U.S. flag, await arrival of Sitkans for potlatch.

CHILKAT INDIANS WAITING FOR THE SITKANS TO ARRIVE TO THE POT

SEAL HERD, St. George Island (May photo, Fourke Fur Co.).

Seal Herd on Increase

At the time of the purchase of Alaska, 1867, the seal herd was estimated to be from three to four million animals. By 1911 uncontrolled slaughter by pelagic sealers reduced the number to 120,000. Seal, like buffalo, were fast becoming extinct, until the Pelagic Treaty between England, United States, Japan and Russian placed them under the protection and jurisdiction of the United States government.

In 1950 the herd was estimated to be over three million seals. World authorities consider this program by the U.S. Fish and Wildlife Service to be one of the greatest achievements in the field of animal conservation.

SALTING DOWN seal skins, left and below (May photo, Fouke Fur Co.).

New Methods Make Better Furs

Fur companies instituted new methods of curing seal skins, to replace the old process by which thousands of skins had been lost through spoilage. The Foulke Fur Company, St. Louis, Mo., as agents of the U.S. Government, the Canadian Government, the Government of South Africa, as well as shippers throughout the world, pioneered this field of processing and sale of fur seal skins.

At dawn from late June to early August the natives go quietly to the grounds which the 'bachelor seals' have chosen. The natives cut off their retreat to the sea and drive them inland. A large group of animals is divided into smaller groups of about fifty seals each, and is surrounded by the natives who select the five-year-olds and allow the rest to leave. After killing and skinning, the pelts are transported by truck to the modern plant on the island.

Here they are quickly cooled, washed free of dirt, blubbered and salted by natives and personnel of the Foulkes company, who go north each spring to supervise the sealing operations.

After the pelts are thoroughly cured in salt, they are packed in barrels for shipment by the government to Seattle and then on to St. Louis. At the Foulke Fur Company they are put through a three-month process involving 125 different operations, most of which require high skill and long experience to create seal skins with faster colors, more permanent and durable, more desirable and supple than in grandmother's time.

90

GOLD SEEKERS camped in the Koyukuk (Hegg photo).

MINERS TEST GRAVEL. News of Kotzebue discovery brought hundreds of gold seekers to that region. Real miners had test boxes of water to sample gravel before working it.

ABRAHAM LINCOLN TOTEM (opposite). Holding Pres. Lincoln in highest esteem, natives gave him honored top place on totem pole in 1882 in old Tongass village. When time weathered features a new Lincoln was carved and placed in Saxman group near Ketchikan. Wind-scarred replica of liberator was preserved in Territorial Museum at Juneau (photo U.S. Forest Service).

Siren Call of Gold

Around 1880 a handful of hardy pioneers staked claims in Turnagain Arm in Resurrection Creek. They elected to winter there, notwithstanding a great scarcity of supplies. When the news of the 'great gold' strike struck Seattle and San Francisco, a mad rush began.

It was a motley crowd that arrived in Cook Inlet that Spring. The majority knew nothing of mining but they would "have gold to throw away in the Fall." They really believed they would pick up all the nuggets they could carry. Of such was the wild fabric stories they told.

But the word "gold" spread farther and farther. Stampeders and those curious about a new land pricked up their ears, heard the call and went.

TOTEMS AND GRAVE POLES at Ketchikan.

GOVERNOR KINCAID, Alaska's first.

Sleeping Giant Stirs

Though the years between 1867-1884 were disorganized years lacking federal attention, in Alaska an undercurrent of interest was beginning to bubble forth. Commanders of military posts at Sitka and Wrangell had administered the law to the best of their ability but it was not enough.

The cry for organized government grew more forceful. Prospectors, sealers, fishermen, whalers and immigrants exploring the coast, the rivers and the interior realized the potential wealth. Under pressure the 84th Congress of the United States presented the 'organic act of 1884' which constituted Alaska as a 'civil and judicial district,' with a governor and skeleton court system.

Sitka was established as the capital. Mining laws were instituted. $25,000 was appropriated for education and the laws of the State of Oregon were extended to Alaska, as far as applicable. John R. Kincaid was appointed Alaska's first governor. His one report to Washington regretted the impossibility to do justice to his job in an isolated district as large as Alaska without laws or assistants or communication.

Governor Swindford (1885-1889), a vigorous organizer who succeeded Gov. Kincaid, gained improvements, government systems, transportation and mail service. He vetoed Oregon laws not suitable to Alaska, and appointed Dr. Sheldon Jackson, a Presbyterian minister, as Commissioner of Education.

HOLY CROSS MISSION, 1900 (Curtis-Miller photo).

Mission Accomplished

Great amazement was expressed by gold-seekers at the appearance of Catholic sisters walking little children or picking berries on a hillside.

Sister May Stephan of the Sisters of St. Ann had arrived at Holy Cross alone, in 1888. Through her efforts a mission was started, and the first sustaining farm in Alaska established. Ground was broken with pointed sticks and smoothed with rakes made by driving nails through boards taken from packing boxes.

Older children had gathered fertilizer from animal trails in the forest. Sister May Stephan, one hundred years old in 1944, mothered thousands of Eskimo and Indian waifs in her orphanage, feeding them largely from her farm. Taught sewing, cooking and sanitation, the older pupils returned in time to the native village to teach a new way of life.

ST. SERGIS CEMETRY on Kuskoquim River, Weather-beaten crosses on many graves tell story of sacrifice and devotion reaching back to Russian regime in 1812. For 100 years light streamed from window of chapel pinpointing place of refuge on stormy nights. Church bells laid benediction on native villages and river voyagers, the wilderness one no longer (Hegg photo, 1900).

U.S. CUTTER *BEAR* (photo Huntington Library).

Mercy Ship of the North

During Alaska's awakening period the Cutter *Bear* joined Alaska's revenue service, flying a flag which signified food, medical care and succour in time of need. Raising the stars and stripes at Sitka could not obliterate a hundred years of cruel Russian tradition and make Alaska American overnight. Only by kindness did natives come to appreciate their new rulers.

The Cutter *Bear* became the best known ship in the cutter service, delivering mail, reindeer, teachers, Eskimos and missionaries to the Arctic. She was a part of two Antarctic expeditions under Admiral Byrd. When forty-eight whaling vessels overstayed summer and were caught in ice floes, the *Bear* came to the rescue.

When Mt. Katmai blew its top in 1912, the *Bear*'s sister ship, the Cutter *Manning*, removed 1500 terror-stricken natives and whites to a safer location. Wherever need arose, Revenue cutters went to the rescue.

CAPT. MICHAEL A. HEALY, commander of revenue cutter *Bear,* at request of Dr. Shelton Jackson, brought many herds of reindeer from Siberia. Many Siberian Eskimos were difficult to deal with, saying "No whiskey— no deer." Missionaries from Sweden, Roman Catholics, Church of England and Moravian stations looked with favor on importation of herds which were boon to Alaskan Eskimos, furnishing milk, meat, skins for clothing, transportation (photo Huntington Museum).

CAPE PRINCE OF WALES
HERD (above)—Nowell-Dudley photo, 1910; left, Laplanders arrive in Seattle (Curtis photo); below, reindeer at Woodland Park, Seattle, en route to Alaska (Asahel Curtis photo).

Reindeer to the Rescue

Dr. Jackson's chief concern as educational agent was the starvation periods among the Eskimos. Through Captain Healey, skipper of the 'Bear,' Dr. Jackson learned of the value of reindeer to the Siberian Eskimo, in furnishing milk, food, clothing, transportation and horn implements.

With the help of Captain Healey, whom the Siberian natives trusted, twenty-one reindeer were brought to Port Clarence. But Eskimos who had lived by hunting and fishing proved they were not herders and Siberian reindeer men had to be brought to teach the Eskimos how to care for the animals.

When this too failed, Lapp reindeer herders were brought from Norway to show the Eskimos the true value of reindeer. To protect the Eskimo in his reindeer venture, the government passed a law forbidding any white man to own a female reindeer.

Dr. Jackson was much pleased with this importation of reindeer to the Arctic regions which had produced a new food supply and so preserved life. It had changed Eskimo hunters to herders and moved them up the scale of civilization.

It had put to good use the thousands of square miles of moss-covered tundra without which reindeer cannot survive. When the increase in the herd was not enough to meet the needs, Dr. Jackson went to Norway to arrange for a larger herd and expert Laplanders to care for them. In 1898 the expedition landed in New York enroute to Seattle with 540 head of reindeer, 418 sleds,

411 sets of harness, bales of reindeer moss, and 115 Laplanders, men, women and children to care for the animals.

With the reindeer herd established on the Alaska tundras, Dr. Jackson began to train young Eskimos in reindeer care under Lapp tutelage. A young man was allowed a few animals a year as pay. At the end of five years he became owner of some forty head, the nucleus of his own herd.

The Laplanders under government contract had a right to request a loan of one hundred head of reindeer for themselves. At the end of three to five years a like number were returned to the government, the Laplanders retaining the increase. The same agreement existed between the missions and the government.

The Laplanders proved to be a valuable addition to the north. Speaking four languages, Lapp, Finnish, Norwegian and Swedish, they soon learned Eskimo, Aleut and English. The tundra became home, the outdoors their habitat.

In a few years the range between Deering and Teller became overstocked. Systematic thinning by the Reindeer Service at the Teller plant was established. 125,000 pounds of reindeer meat shipped in cold storage to New York was well received and reindeer raising along the Arctic seas became a permanent industry.

In 1913 restrictions on White ownership of reindeer was removed. Carl Lomen, Jofet Lindeberg and Dr. J. H. Mustard of Nome entered the business as Lomen & Company. By 1930 reindeer herds totalled over one million animals.

REINDEER AT WOODLAND PARK, Seattle; Expedition from Norway arrived safely in Seattle where animals were rested, then transported with Laplanders on cutter *Bear* to various parts of Alaska (Asahal Curtis photo); below, Laplanders milking reindeer (Hegg photo, 1900).

LASSOING REINDEER (Asahel Curtis photo).

WHALER *FEARLESS* caught
in Arctic Ocean ice.

DEERING, Alaska (above), Nowell photo, 1903.

PETERSBURG CANNERY (left), photo Curtis & Miller.

Education Meant Work

When the missionary, Rev. N. O. Hultberg, was sent to Deering and the Arctic to organize some form of industrial work among the Eskimos to prevent periods of starvation, he changed the previous system of education. Schools had been established but how could confining boys and girls in a school room during the fishing and hunting season prevent starvation later on?

Every member of the Eskimo family must do his part to ensure survival. Common sense dictated the importation of fishing tackle, whaling tools and boom guns to replace their awkward lances and spears. In appreciation the natives took Rev. Hultberg to their hearts.

Fear of the 'outside man' vanished and the natives talked freely of their resources. Deering was to gain when Rev. Hultberg learned of great deposits of 'black rock' (coal) now so important since steam was replacing the sail. They brought him 'pretty yellow rocks' from a gold prospect which later netted him $5,000 to the ton in San Francisco and caused the stampede of a thousand people to the Kotzebue region.

THLINGET PACKING COMPANY fish trap (Roger Dudley photo).

Gunboat Disturbs Peace

Fish now rivaled furs in importance in the north Pacific. Fish traps bridged every river and canneries stood on spindly legs in a neighboring cove.

In 1892 Russia dipped her fingers into this rich fish barrel by enforcing a tax or license on all vessels fishing outside the 30-mile offshore limit. The climax came in 1907 when a Russian gunboat passed along the fishing banks and placed all fishing boats under arrest, confiscated their papers and ordered them to sea.

Bewildered angry captains tossed the international question into the lap of Uncle Sam. The Secretary of State rendered the decision that international law granted the boats a three-mile limit and Russian gunboats were ordered to the fishing banks to return the papers to the ships.

However, 'King Salmon' remained a favored product and large modern canneries blossomed along the coast, drawing upon native population for its labor. Fish being their way of life since time immemorial, the natives were interested, skilled and quick in cleaning and processing salmon.

The value of the salmon 'take' varies from year to year, but averages about $80,000,000 per annum. The largest cannery in the world was built at Karluk where 1100 employees canned over 200,000 tins containing three million salmon per year. A single haul in this river netted 17,000 salmon, with thousands left to die on the banks and bars.

TROPHIES FROM KENAI PENINSULA (Kluckholm photo).

Hunters Find Paradise

While the majority of Americans still considered Alaska an ice-covered wilderness, to hunters it was happy ground. City parks clamored for polar bears, grizzly cubs, mountain sheep and moose for their zoos.

Taxidermists wanted moose heads, deer and caribou heads with a wide spread of antlers for hotel lobbies and lodges. Soon patrons of museums gazed wide-eyed at mammoth Kodiak bears, reared up on their hind legs, while a white polar bear rug with snarling mouth became a prized possession to the elite. And proud indeed was the owner who had shot the trophy himself, shot it on the ice floes near the North Pole while stalking a herd of walrus.

Newspapers kept alive the story of big bears, big fish, big moose and the trophy gave proof of its veracity.

BOARDING HOUSE at Perserverence Mine (Case photo).

New Industry in North

Fishermen and prospectors brought news of the mountains of quartz, granite and marble near Ketchikan suitable as building stones for the growing cities to the south.

Modern hotels in the growing cities of Seattle, Portland and San Francisco boasted polished marble walls and winding stairways. Citizens pointed with pride to their civic buildings and tycoons on the hill had stone steps and marble halls. Tombstones etched with angels, cherubs and scripture rose above the new-made graves or replaced weathered headboards.

As the demand increased, modern machinery was installed and the migration of miners brought new interest to Alaska calling prospectors to the hills for new wealth.

Rumors of gold along the Pacific Coast drew George Pitz, a mining engineer, in 1880. Wooing the natives in Sitka he promised a hundred pairs of Hudson's Bay blankets and work for the tribe at a dollar a day for a worthwhile ore sample.

Before long Chief Koweek, chief of the Auks, appeared bearing samples of gold-veined quartz and news, "Whole mountain, she all gold."

Immediately Pitz sent the prospectors Juneau and Harris paddling to the prospect in the little bay to investigate. They climbed the mountain, probing the worthless white out-croppings as they climbed. From the summit deep down in a ravine on the other side flowed a stream dotted with huge quartz boulders. They clamored down and stopped speechless on the bank. The white quartz gleamed in a filigree of gold, dimpled with nuggets as large as nuts. Feverishly they set to work and in a few days dug out $14,000. Then the 'grub' ran out. But a new gold strike had been made.

MARBLE QUARRIES at Dolomi near Ketchikan (above and 3 photos below)—Kluckholm photo.

GLORY HOLE, Treadwell mine (above)—(Curtis & Miller photo).

UNDERGROUND AT TREADWELL MINE (above left and center), (Curtis & Miller photo).

GLORY HOLE, Treadwell mine (Curtis & Miller photo).

Gold in the Virgin Land

Pierre Crussard, a Franch-Canadian prospector known as French Pete was living among the Indians at Sitka when Juneau and Harris returned with the news of their gold discovery. French Pete left immediately with his Indians on a prospect of their own. Poking around offshore on Douglas Island he found an outcropping of gold-bearing quartz which he called his 'Paris claim.'

STAMP MILL at Treadwell (Curtis & Miller photo).

Sluicing on Paris claim paid fairly well, proved to be hard work, and no bonanza, so he sold out for $500 to John Treadwell, a contractor with some mining experience in Nevada. Treadwell liked the prospect, went to San Francisco and bought a five-stamp mill. The Alaska Treadwell Mining Company was formed in 1880. In time, 880 stamps were treating 360,000 tons of ore yielding $3,250,000 a year and it was said the "glory hole" was so deep, men working at the bottom seemed scarcely larger than flies.

Mine workings that bore into the inner chambers some five hundred forty feet below look like the tunneling of a mole. Cages descend the shafts, stopping at stations from which galleries lead through solid rock.

A train of cars, filled with ore rattles along the tiny railroad track. Ascending a short ladder to a cavernous opening, one is reminded of the Catacombs of early Rome. Here by dimly lit candles men are working. The great chamber, 180 feet wide and 100 feet long, is divided by pillars 18 to 25 feet thick so that the entire underground exca-

vation might be 200 feet wide and 500 feet long. Shadows make gnomes of the men and chugging machine drills fill the vaults with sound.

The Treadwell mine which fed the largest stamp mill in the world was to become justly famous.

Like 10,000 Thors wielding 10,000 hammers on 10,000 anvils, the 800 stamps roared across Gastineau channel without ceasing. The stamp falls on the die, like a hammer on an anvil, crushes the pieces of ore and releases the gold as the kernel of a nut is released. When the ore is thoroughly pulverized, it is sluiced over copper plate covered with mercury, which catches the gold.

Each stamp pulverizes to powder five and a half tons of ore in twenty-four hours. A stamp mill is a place of thunderous power so full of roaring that voices are completely lost in the rhythmic reverberations and the roaring echoes far beyond the confines of the mill, drawing upon that restless breed of men who are forever searching fortune in virgin land.

107

JUNEAU, 1880

Rush to Juneau

The discovery of gold near Juneau drained the American continent, the Cassiar and the Cariboo of Canada of prospectors. Chinese laborers abandoned along the Telegraph line, left the Cassiar country in such quick migration that Juneau became largely Chinese.

Whites objected. Fights, riots and persecution followed until in 1886 citizens herded the 'celestials' onto schooners outward bound—all except China Joe who had endeared himself to the whites in the Cassiar.

For forty years Alaska was ruled, or mis-ruled, by the discarded Deady code of Oregon. In 1899 a criminal code was enacted and with it came a business and trade tax to support city government. In 1900 the capitol was transferred from Sitka to Juneau and Alaska civil code superseded the obsolete Oregon code.

However, progress in Alaska made constant revision of the land laws necessary and the possibility of home government by Alaskans themselves became a burning issue.

ROAD TO JUNEAU (top) gold mines; center, barge unloading at Mt. Andrew Dock.

PRESBYTERIAN CHURCH at Juneau. Various religious orders sent missionaries to Alaska. They built churches, established schools, lived life of sacrifice. Little by little their work took hold and in times of stress unfortunates found candles burning in windows, latchstrings on outside.

I Am Gold . . .

I AM GOLD, the mystery of the ages. From time immemorial I have been sought by men in all lands. My value, defined by no one, increased by time, has been constant for thousands of years.

I am the great gift of Mother Earth.

Men perish to reach me. Men shoot to take me, steal from those who find me. I build cities. I am a philanthropist I buy milk and diamonds, flowers and baubles. I help the sick and bury the dead.

I am the great lure, appealing to young and old. I was 3,000 years old when Christ was born. Men suffer to reach me and when they own me they lose me. Spendthrifts fling me and I am a comfort to the aged.

I am a wanderer, passing from hand to hand without a home, now being used for good, now evil but *always* representing value. Strong nations are my friends and hoard me. Weak nations fear and belittle me but all want me.

I am the dream of youth, the appetite of the avaricious, and the sorrow of those who lost me. I kindle the brain, awaken the imagination and spur men on to their goal.

I am gold!

(Author Unknown)

Gold! Gold! Gold!

A financial depression was creeping over the country to the south,—the United States and Europe. By 1893 there was no mistake of it. In western United States the railroads laid off their crews and men walked the tracks they laid, begging food at the cook shacks. Logging camps turned their teams to pasture. People lived largely by barter and trade.

But the forests furnished bear and deer, pheasants and ducks and the sea gave clams and fish. So men took their fishing poles and guns. There was no welfare. The abundance from one family fed his neighbor.

Indians, even such as Princess Evangeline, Chief Sealth's daughter, washed clothes for the "white ladies" and the Indians traded clams, birds and perhaps a piece of venison for a pan or old dress.

How long would it last? No one knew as the years slipped slowly by.

Then Gold! Gold! Gold! A ton of gold arrived on the *S. S. Portland* from the Klondike! Before the summer was over the *S. S. Excelsior* came; and the *Humbolt*, each with $750,000 in yellow raw gold. Three tons of Klondike gold! Nuggets in the grass roots! Scooped from creek beds! Six months or a year made a millionaire!

But where was the Klondike? In Canada? In Alaska? No one knew. You sailed up the Pacific Coast to Dyea or Skagway. You clawed your way over the mountains, then 'floated' down the Yukon 600 miles to Dawson where the Klondike met the Yukon.

Among the hills, the creeks with the gold bottoms poured into the Klondike. Gone now was the panic of '93. Gone the bartering of eggs and potatoes for sugar and flour, of trading shingle bolts for shoes. Money appeared as mysteriously as it had disappeared in the baffling hard times of 1893.

All eyes focussed on the gold fields—Canada, United States, England, Australia and the world. Like a swarm of locusts, gold seekers descended on the seaport towns along the Pacific Coast, enroute to a place where "gold lay like chicken feed on the surface of the ground."

For four years crowds surged about the docks seeking passage to Dyea, Skagway, or St. Michael.

The *Excelsior*, the *Portland*, the *Alki*, the *Topeka*, *Willamette*, and others, loaded with gold-crazed stampeders, grubstakes, horses, and hay, shuttled up and down

111

the Alaskan Coast, followed by an armada of sailing vessels, launches, fishing boats and tugs towing top-heavy scows. Unseaworthy boats were manned by crews who had never heard of "williwaws," tide rips or the churning waters which lashed the rock strewn coastline. Men stormed ticket offices begging passage, offering to pay fabulous prices for tickets already sold. And steamship companies desperate for this new surge of business, searched the far seas for additional vessels. Men who could not go, dipped their fingers into the pot of gold by grubstaking those who could. Meanwhile, information concerning this new treasure house was scant and scattered. Even the boundary line between Canada and Alaska had not been officially surveyed. The discovery of gold raised the question: "Where is this Klondike?" The United States claimed the region by right of purchase. Canada claimed it by right of settlement. While thousands joined the wild stampede, two great countries wrestled with the problems of establishing the boundary line.

STEAMER *WILLAMETTE* at Seattle bound for Yukon in '98 (Curtis & Miller photo); below, fortune seekers crowd steamer for Skagway and points north.

YESLER STREET at First Avenue, Seattle, 1899 (Asahel Curtis photo).

Seattle Business Boomed

The Klondike gold strike revived business along the Pacific Coast and across the nation. Freight piled up along the streets of Seattle. New industries were born, making tin dishes, parkas, clothes, Klondike stores, etc. Shipbuilders laid the hulls of river steamers.

Trains shuttled east and west along new lines of steel, loaded with stampeded goods. Steamers, schooners, whalers, and derelicts of the sea sailed for Alaska.

In a year's time miners arrived from the gold fields, dripping with nuggets, stick pins, cufflinks and nugget watch chains draped across the vest. And the nuggets and the stories told, blotted out the failures who had slunk back to the old job at the mill but the north was no longer unimportant nor unknown. Men began to shift their eyes from the Klondike to that unmeasured place called 'Alaska.'

MINERS ARRIVING on steamer *Excelsior* with their gold created stir in San Francisco. Here was proof there was gold in the North—the full realization of enormity of Klondike discovery. 3 steamers—*Excelsior, Humboldt, Portland* brought in a ton of gold each and news flashed across the country, across world (Asahel Curtis photo).

GEORGE CARMACK   SKOOKUM JIM   BOB HENDERSON

GEORGE CARMACK standing beside 1904 car in North
Bend, Wash.

KATE CARMACK

MUD FLATS OF DYEA, Alaska, where hopefuls landed with their supplies—flour, bacon, milk, dried fruit, tents, stoves, bed rolls, blankets.

Carmack Party Found First Klondike Gold

George Carmack, Kate his wife, Skookum Jim, her brother, and Tagish Charlie, had gone down the Yukon prospecting and fishing. They stopped to fish at the mouth of the Klondike. Here Bob Henderson met and talked with them, suggesting they prospect up the Klondike. Later they did move up the Klondike, camping on Rabbit Creek. While getting water from Bonanza Creek, Kate found the glitterings of gold shining in the bottom of the creek. So was gold discovered, the story told to this author by Mrs. Florence Hartshorn, a good personal friend of Kate Carmack.

Gold was everywhere in the muck and creek beds. $1400 was sluiced out in a few days. Then Carmack staked out a claim, and one for Skookum Jim and one for Tagish Charlie.

After some months Kate Carmack grew tired of confusion along the Klondike and finally returned to Cariboo Crossing where she was raised.

George Carmack "sold out" his Bonanza claims and went to Seattle, Washington, later to prospect and stake claims in the mountains beyond North Bend in that state and build a city to be called "Alaska."

Bonanza Claims By Carmack, Skookum Jim
and Tagish Charley

Discovery staked by George Carmack
1 Below Discovery by George Carmack
2 Below Discovery staked by Tagish Charley
2 Below Discovery staked by Tagish Charley
1 Above Discovery staked by Tagish Jim

On August 2, 1900 Carmack sold Discovery and No. 1 Below to Tagish Jim for $20,000.00.

Tagish Jim sold one-third of No. 1 Above Discovery to G. D. Bently for $10,000.00. Later bought it back for $20,000.00

Tagish Jim finally sold Discovery, No. 1 Above and No. 1 Below to the Lewis River Mining and Dredging Company for $65,000.00.

Tagish Charley sold No. 2 Below Discovery:

Undivided half to P. G. MacDonald
Undivided half to J. C. Tabor
Undivided half to R. E. Edgar
Undivided half to G. T. Edgar

In the records Jim signs Tagish Jim but he was commonly known as Skookum Jim.

115

ASCENDING CHILKOOT MOUNTAIN (See frontis-piece) Hegg photo, 1897.

Pass to Pandemonium

Into the mountains, up the well-worn Indian trail, across the creeks, through the canyons, to Sheep Camp, the Scales, they moved in a never-ending line toward the Yukon River. Over Chilkoot Mountain they struggled, lugging 100 lbs. at a time, sack of flour, box of bacon, case of milk—food, a tent, a stove. Storms, blizzards, rain, wili-was and fatigue would stop a host of them.

CAMP DYEA—"And not a man among them who knew the hazards that lay ahead."

"MEXICAN HITCH." Cruelty to pack horses was unspeakable. Young Mexican showed stampeders how to build pack so it would not slip or slide.

WHITE PASS TRAIL out of Skagway where over 3,000 horses fell. Starved, overloaded, snow-blinded, weak, their bodies formed part of trail (Asahel Curtis photo).

SKAGWAY, ALASKA (Hegg photo, 1898).

CUSTOMS OFFICIALS on White Pass Trail. Two flags wave on summit of trail. Discovery of gold raised international question—"Was Klondike in Alaska or Canada?"

Back Door to Riches

Some stampeders landed at Skagway six miles from Dyea, on the mudflats at the end of Lynn Canal, dashed over the Moore Homestead and Skagway was born. Into the mountains they scurried to set first feet in the fabulous Bonanza.

Relaying 'grub,' crossing bouldered streams waist deep with ice-cold water, hurrying on mile after mile—sweating, hungry, dying. No time to sleep! No time to eat! The race was not over until they dipped their fingers in that pot of gold.

Skagway boomed—thrived and feared under the rule of 'Soapy' Smith. By 1898 wharves penciled the muddy tide flat. By 1900 a railroad gyrated through the White Pass connecting the sea with river transportation, and Skagway was assured permanency.

King Midas had pried open a back door leading into Alaska.

TRAIL OF '98 ran along mountainside where there was hardly footing for pack animal (Larss & Duclos photo, 1898).

WHITE PASS & YUKON RAILROAD, 110 miles long, was completed in 1900 thru Canadian and U.S. territory, first railroad in Alaska. Close Bros. of England, with Michael Heney as construction engineer, saw ahead to day when gold rush would end and north find normal economic growth (Hegg photo, 1900).

"STRIKE AT ATLIN!" (above left). Atlin district lay some 75 miles south of White Pass & Yukon Railroad. Workers threw down tools and left jobs to find gold, engineer Michel Heney sending frantic calls to Seattle for replacements.

E. A. HEGG, who made many of photographs in this volume, with P. B. Anderson, his helper Swan and brother Ed, camped on shore of Yukon. Hegg was one of first photographers to follow gold rush in '97. From Dawson he went to Nome and Guggenheim interests in Cordova. When he left Dawson he sold out to Larss who carried on his work.

AT LAKE BENNETT (above center and right) gold-hungry men stopped only long enoug to build boats and scows—or coffins—to take them down Yukon River. 10,000 boat builders biggest boat-building center of north! All most men had was ingenuity, to fall trees, whipsa lumber, drag it to lake shore, fashion boat perhaps with hands that had never held hamme 800 feet of lumber was needed for boat suitable of carrying ton of freight . . . but gold-glaze eyes visioned only dust to be shaken from grass roots of Klondike (Hegg, 1898).

"ALL ABOARD!" (right) on raft of logs—Klondike-Bound. Bottom, Yukon ingenuity contrived this stern-wheeler.

STERN-WHEELER *MONARCH* loading cordwood for fuel on Yukon.

AT TAGISH, post for mounted police, mail was dumped on ground and each man picked out his own.

MILES CANYON and White Horse Rapids which stampeders were forced to go thru in 1897 and 1898. Pilots charged $25 which many did not have. One McCauley built tram line around Miles Canyon and the Rapids charging 5¢ a pound for hauling freight (Hegg photo).

SAIL ON LAKE LE BARGE (Larss & Duclos photo).

SUPPLY STORES (above, left, opposite top) held all manner of goods as thousands of stampeders sold out grub stakes for fare home.

"Here we are . . . Where are we?"

They arrived—the strong, the lucky—at Dawson, shouldered their packs and trudged up the Klondike to Bonanza, Bear Creek, Hunker and Sulphur, poking their fingers into the rich pay dirt of the Eldorado.

They watched the sluice boxes at clean-up time. A migration of 50,000 people for 10,000 claims. Gold in every sluice box but no gold for thousands. No gold on top of the ground. No gold in the grass roots. They had come too late.

So many went to work for wages and the fare back home. Others pioneered the wilderness, still hoping to find a creek with a 'gold bottom.'

SUPPLY STORES and below, gold seekers, in Dawson (Larss & Duclos photo).

DAWSON CITY, 1897-8 (Hegg photo, 1898).

WINDLASS on El Dorado Creek.

YUKON NATIVE with malamutes.

"DOG DIRTY" and loaded for bear.

FOOD CACHE near Fairbanks.

Spell of the Yukon

In the Klondike district the ground was frozen to bedrock at depths ranging from fifteen to forty feet below the surface. This forced miners to devise new methods of mining, as previous experiences in other camps were of little benefit. The first miners used wood fires to sink their shafts to bedrock. A fire about six feet long and four feet wide was built on the ground and allowed to burn eight or ten hours, then ground which was thawed, was dug out. Another fire was started in the hole, followed in ten hours by another excavation. By alternate thawing and digging, the shaft was sunk to bedrock at the rate of two or three feet for each fire. In most cases cribbing becomes necessary. When bedrock was reached, the miner began to drift by continued means of fire, hoisting out the gravel and bedrock formation containing the gold. Shaft sinking and drifting were done in winter. As soon as the ice melted in the spring, sluicing was begun. Miners soon replaced fires for thawing, with steam points and steam generated by a boiler at the surface.

CLEAN UP TIME (top 3 photos) on No. 16 Eldorado.

PACKING OUT THE GOLD (opposite and right). Each pack horse carried about $20,000, pack train perhaps $100,000 after clean up. Shipments were always guarded by police and owners, gold stored with reliable firms in Dawson until shipped on first available boat. In Dawson and along creeks, gold was used as legal tender, each man carrying poke of dust which was weighed on scales in payment for purchases. All nickles, dimes, pennies were tossed in box behind counter for nothing sold that cheaply (Curtis photos).

MINERAL HOT SPRINGS, Bonanza (Hegg photo).

CHECHACO HILL

GOLD HILL on Bonanza Creek was literally turned "inside out" as piles of tailings grew.

Gold Deposit . . . Why and Where

Why was Bonanza gold dark?

Why was Eldorado gold, nearby, bright and shiny?

Why does gold lay in yellow ribbons deep down, where streams could not possibly carry it? Why is some solid quartz formation filigreed with gold deposit while nearby in a quartz district, gold lays free and there is no quartz?

This author, after much study, presents this possible solution, based on the proximity of gold quartz to lime deposits, and the slanting strata of rock formation:

We must begin in prehistoric times, during the period of upheaval of mountain ranges, when huge deposits of gold-bearing quartz were tossed up from the very bowels of the earth. In the earth's convulsion, this quartz might have come from widely separated places where quartz was impregnated with gold, pure as in Bonanza gold, or impregnated with gold and tin or alloy, as in Eldorado gold. In the upheaval, the earth's strata of various rock formations is twisted and slanting.

Limestone formation associates itself with placer mining. In many parts of the north, hot springs laden with various mineral solutions bubble to the surface.

Is it not possible that rains and surface water following a slanting strata penetrates the earth and combining with a lime deposit generates heat enough to dissolve the dissolvable minerals such as quartz?

This hot flow which we call 'hot springs' forced by pressure to the surface, contains various minerals such as sulphur, sodium phosphate, etc., in solution. Now should there be gold embedded in the quartz dissolved deep in the earth, the gold being insoluble, would be freed and dropped. Gold might still be imprisoned in the quartz which was beyond the reach of limestone heat. In some localities the earth strata does not permit water to reach a lime deposit, or perhaps lime is absent, and hence we have hard rock mining and the necessity of freeing the gold in stamp mills.

SLUICING WINTER'S WORK on claims No. 58, 59, 60 and 61 below Discovery on Bonanza (Hegg photo).

DOG TEAM running out of Dawson. Dog was to Alaska what covered wagon, pack horse were to California '49ers. Load for each dog was approximately 150 pounds. If in good shape he could carry it for 8 hours. Always ready when needed for work, dog did his share in settling country, enduring same hardships as prospector. In many cases he furnished food for him, often died with him, and in one case made gold discovery while digging rabbit out of root hole (Hegg photo).

"WHAT COLOR WE GOT, PARDNER?" Sluice box on Gold Hill (Curtis photo).

NEW ZEALANDER'S CABIN near Dawson (Larss & Duclos photo).

WHIPSAWING LUMBER for Klondike cabin (Curtis photo).

PHOTOGRAPHERS HEGG and Larss set out on picture-taking trip.

CANADIAN DEVELOPMENT DOCK at Dawson.

DAWSON, 1900 (Hegg photo).

FIRE IN DAWSON. City had several serious fires because houses, heated by wood, were tinder dry. In above photo, when dance hall girl threw lamp at another girl. It fired town. Yukon River was frozen 5 feet deep and with hoses frozen there was no water. Alaska Commercial Co., fearing for food supply, irreplaceable in winter, put blankets over buildings and doused them with beer which did not freeze.

DAWSON, 30 years after gold rush showing dredge tailings on Klondike River, Between 1896 and 1900, 50,000 people landing at Dawson made muskeg swamp into well organized city. By 1900 first rare atmosphere of stampede was over. Gold seekers were absorbed into city life. Mining corporations, dredges and modern machinery then took over. Between 1898 and 1905 Klondike creeks produced $100 million within 15 mile radius.

CABIN ON BONANZA CREEK (Hegg photo).

LARGEST NUGGET ever found in Alaska, 97 oz. and valued at $1,552, found at Pioneer Mining Co.'s Anvil Creek mine, Sept. 14, 1901 (Hegg photo).

On to Nome

Prospectors and men disappointed in the Dawson, pushed out into the northern wilderness in increasing numbers. One by one these settled at the confluence of rivers or went on to prospect. The Klondike coming when it did obliterated the depression of 1893 and business flowed furiously once more.

While gold was being mined by prospectors along the various creeks of the seven hundred mile tundra of Seward Peninsula, it was the discovery on Anvil Creek in 1898 by "the three Swedes"—Lindeberg, Lindholm and Bryntesen—that rekindled the fire set by Carmack in the Klondike. Vague were the ideas about the Nome country. A barren, desolate, treeless region where Eskimoes lived in "ice block houses and blizzards rioted through a long winter." But here was a gold strike as good as Carmack's.

Taking with them the $50 which they had panned out in a few days, they decided to winter over in Golovin Bay keeping their discovery a secret. Since they must organize the district which was necessary, the news leaked out and other prospectors from the Kotzbue district rushed in. However, the Cape Nome Mining District was organized, including G. W. Price, a miner from California, a Dr. Kittilsen, a government physician for the Laplanders who cared for reindeer and S. Tornensis. They restaked the ground to comply with the law and called a miners' meeting to enact local laws to govern the entire district.

When the miners went "out" in the fall of 1899, with $3,000,000 worth of gold, a gold stampede was on all over again. $3,000,000, a new Eldorado!

During the first season in spite of ground freezing and snow falling, miners succeeded in panning and rocking out $1,800 in a few days. No attempt was made to work the ground that winter but in the spring they came to have a look at the new bonanza which had been found.

The first prospectors to arrive had honored mining laws—knew the district was organized and had regulations, one of which was the right of location by agent or attorney. Also, the discoverer of a claim was entitled to Discovery claim and one other, usually chosen adjoining his discovery claim. Other claims were designated as "one above discovery" or "two below" and so on.

Because of previous work among Eskimos such as missionary work and reindeer supervising, Scandinavians were among the first to stake claims in the Seward Peninsula. Now, these not being naturalized citizens according to the newcomers, were held not eligible to hold claims. This news caused a rush to the seven thousand acres of rich placer ground already staked by these aliens.

Claims were jumped recklessly, rejumped until some claims were covered by relocations three and four deep. Litigation, gun fights, and near-murder followed. Miners defied newcomers with guns. Anarchy prevailed where there was no law except by unscrupulous lawyers and the military at St. Michaels who had no legal authority to interfere, and Washington, D.C., six thousand miles away.

The tundra now swarmed with stampeders staking claims on ground already staked by mining districts recently organized. Mine owners sent to the military post at St. Michaels for help and General Randall established Lt. Spaulding with a squad of soldiers at Nome in the event that he might be needed to preserve order.

When new arrivals, American citizens from the south, came they objected furiously that the most valuable property had been staked by aliens—Eskimos and Swedes who had rushed in (to stake claims) using government reindeer for transportation. They demanded a law restricting a man to one claim; that the district be properly organized by the government; the original staking be declared illegal because a person locating more than one claim on a creek threw the property open to relocation.

The greatest need in the Nome tundras was timber and wood. Except for a board washed up on the beach or the tangled trees at the mouth of the Yukon, the country was absolutely treeless.

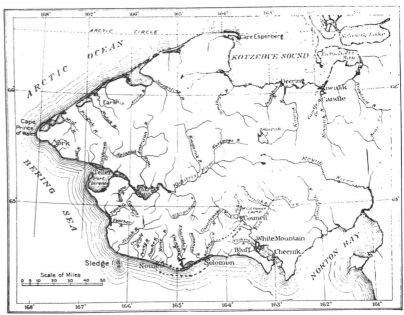

THE SEWARD PENINSULA.
Illustrating Route from Nome to Ophir.

Gold Rush Country

Seward Peninsula comprises an area of 22,700 square miles. A tundra about five miles wide extends back from the sea to low rounding hills. Thirty miles beyond these treeless hills, the Sawtooth Mountains knife the skies. Streams flow in all directions. Spring suddenly spreads a flowered green carpet over the hills and night is no more from May until September. Quite baffling is that long day when work never ceases and sleep refuses to come. Stifling, too, is a land which is isolated and ice-locked for eight long months.

Prior to the gold rush, Seward Peninsula, a barren desolate region, was visited only spasmodically by a few traders and missionaries.

There was gold here and silver, coal and tin. Anvil Creek, a branch of the Snake River, not shown on the above map, is located north and east of Nome.

ANVIL CITY in Nome area where gold was discovered by Lindeberg, Lindholm and Bryntesen in 1898. Rex Beach used site for his novel, *The Spoilers* (Hegg photo).

CLEAN UP ON NO. 1, Daniels Creek (Hegg photo). CALIFORNIA BENCH on Glacier Creek (Hegg photo).

SHIPMENT TO NOME from John B. Agen Co. in Seattle waiting for transfer to ship.

ON GLACIER

FIRST ARRIVALS at Anvil used Eskimo barabaras built of sod. In all expanse of tundra there was no tree, no shrub larger than willow whip, not a board, not a log except tangled piles of driftwood on delta of Yukon River (Hegg photo).

SURF AT NOME (Hegg photo).

141

BLUFF CITY. Over 500 men washed out $2 million in gold by means of rockers, 30 miles of beach being worked at one time. In 3 days two partners cleaned up $4,000. In 1900 resident of St. Michael came to Nome with two old rockers. He leased them on royalty basis of 50% of all gold rocked by his machines and in 2 weeks he made $2,800 (Hegg photo).

BOATS filled with supplies for Nome at Council City on Nekluk River.

FRONT STREET, Nome. By July 1, 1900, street was blockaded with people and teams. . . . "Where do we go? Where do we eat? Where do we sleep?"

ROCKING ON BEACH at Bluff City (Hegg photo).

Rocking for Riches

On Golovin Bay beaches, miners rocked out as much as 130 ounces a day. At $35 an ounce, some "got rich quick" taking out some $40,000 in the short 4 months of the summer season. The strip of sandy beach was theirs only as long as they stayed and worked it and as long as the weather was calm, for a Behring storm might re-concentrate the gold deposit and move it to the beach strip of his neighbor many feet away.

No filing of a beach claim was possible under the law that "ground washed by the Behring Sea at extreme high tide was government reservation."

Each man held a small strip of ground only as long as he stayed there and worked it. Though there were numerous "long toms" there was little disorder among the first locators. Each man knew his rights and held to them.

The district back to the tundra was divided into the First, Second and Third beaches. "Ruby sand" a mixture of sand and granules of garnet defined the First beach at the tide limit with a reddish band. Second and Third beaches lay back on the tundra.

4TH OF JULY PARADE on Stedman Avenue, Nome, 1901. Beneath frantic stampede for gold, Nome was building for permanency. By 1904 telephone system, long distance lines connected Nome with teller, Council and Cheenik, and plans were made for extension to connect Unalaska with U.S. Government telegraph line (Hegg photo).

GOLD BRICKS at Bank of Cape Nome—about 1,000 ounces each (Hegg photo).

BEACH AT NOME—June 28, 1900 (Hegg photo).

The Sands Ran Red

The Nome beach looking west was a conglomeration of freight by June 1900. Never in the history of a mining camp had there been such wholesale staking of claims. They staked beaches, and creeks, then spread out into the country staking without regard for laws or filing. Claims were jumped. Disputes followed. Many of the decisions handed down by the Federal Court did not make for peace. It was a lawyer's paradise. One hundred sixteen attorneys-at-law were registered with the clerk of the court, fifty-one of whom were in active practice.

Much of the gold in the beach was found in layers of ruby sand. The depth to bedrock, mean-low-water to the tundra was one-hundred-fifty feet.

Barges were used to relay passengers and freight. In 1901 more than 150,000 tons of freight was landed on the beach at Nome and more than 15,000 people accompanied these miscellaneous cargoes. The distance from Seattle to Nome is 2,350 miles, and steamers make the trip in about eight days.

Crates of merchandise, lumber, household goods, kegs of beer, barrels of whiskey, steam thaw-boilers, made a grand disorder. Out over the tundra men dragged lumber and mining machinery to their claims. Great sheet-iron warehouses of the Northern Commercial Company took shape at the edge of the tundra. Saloons never closed their doors in the long day. Gold dust flowed like a river over the bars and beer barrels cluttered the streets. Bustle and excitement filled the air while gold was being sifted from the beach sands for forty miles and more.

MIDNIGHT SUN gave light to Nome through summer but lamplit winters were long and dark until artificial lighting was supplied by electric light plant of Pioneer Mining Co. (Hegg photo).

144

LIGHTERING GOODS with derrick, Nome (Hegg photo).

Many Never Left the Ships

Prior to the gold rush only the occasional ship stopped for trading purposes at St. Michaels on Seward Peninsula. Now at Nome the passenger received his initiation into the difficulties of transportation in the North.

Since there was no pier, a little tug towing a big black barge steamed out to the ship. If the sea was calm, the passengers walked a gang plank to land. If stormy the new arrivals were hoisted from the barge with a derrick and boom and slung through the air to a platform at the water's edge.

Goods and passengers were lightered in on scows and small crafts. In 1900 some twenty-thousand stampeders arrived in Nome in one-hundred-sixty-two steamers and seventy-five sailing vessels. Ice blocks the sea eight months of the year while violent storms make shipping perilous.

There was no law, no order. Many never left the ship. One look at the barren countryside was enough—gold or no gold.

Yet in the summer of 1900 thirty-five-thousand people landed in Nome hoping for quick riches. The high cost of living, poor quarters or none, lack of work coupled with an epidemic of smallpox, stories of blizzards and freezing winters discouraged so many they left almost immediately, selling outfits for what they could get.

PROSPERITY REIGNED in Nome. Disillusioned had gone home leaving land to pioneer and "lucky ones".

WINTER ON FRONT STREET, Nome (Nowell photo).　　　　　ANVIL MASONIC CLUB SOCIAL

ARRIVAL OF CAPT. AMUNDSEN Front row (1) Capt. Amundsen (2) Lieut. Hansen
(Nowell, 1906).

Explorer Amundsen Returns

Nome, Alaska, sunned herself in world noto-riety again in 1906 when Capt. Amundsen pi-loted the sloop *Agjoa* into the roadstead on Sept. 1, 1906. After three years of Arctic exploration, he had discovered the Northwest Passage, an honor sought by nations for thirty years.

Nome's welcome to the Norwegian captain and crew was riotous. The Norwegian national an-them, played by Nome's brass band, welcomed them ashore! There were cheers, handshakes and congratulations. Later there were feasts and

toasts. The news was relayed to Norway and an interested world traced the coastline of Alaska to locate a city called Nome, the first to welcome the *Agjoa* and its crew.

Discovery of the Northwest Passage was Capt. Amundsen's greatest achievement though in an-other year he reached the South Pole by dog team.

In 1912 Nome honored Mr. Stephanssen en-route to further Arctic exploration and this time Nome was easier to pinpoint.

LIGHTERING GOLD, Nome (Nowell photo).

"Hundred Days' War"

The $1,200,000 in gold bought by the Miners and Merchants Bank of Nome in 1902 was only part of the winter's clean-up. The average output of $5,000,000 annually does not indicate a fabulous wealth until we consider that the mining season runs but one hundred days a year. $648,000,000 worth of gold—and silver—were produced in the Nome region between 1899 and 1905.

In order to catch the fine gold, quick silver which amalgamates with free gold, is sprinkled along the riffles of the sluice boxes and rockers. Later, this amalgam is placed in a retort which separates the quick silver for re-use.

Gold bricks at the bank piled up and were shipped out to the States. In 1907 Nome boasted as many as four hundred dogs. To feed this number was quite a problem. When the last boat to Nome failed to bring money, there was no folding money for winter's use. In cooperation with the bank Mr. A. G. Simmer designed and printed paper money to be used until spring opened the seaways. On a $1 bill was the head of a "husky" dog; on a $5 bill an Eskimo man; on a $10 bill an Eskimo woman; and on a $20 bill appeared an ice hummock. These passed as legal tender. "Most people get jailed for making counterfeit money, you get paid for it," Nome told Mr. Simmer.

DREDGING on Snake River, Nome.

SCHOOL CHILDREN, Nome (Hegg photo).

Nome Was Home to Billy Mitchell

Many famous people have walked the streets of Nome, Alaska. A few attended her schools. One was 'Billy' Mitchell who rose to the rank of General in the U.S. Air Force, was decorated by France, honored by England, and held in highest esteem by General Pershing.

Billy Mitchell grew up in Nome, Alaska, no doubt he played on the beaches and gazed across the sea to Siberia. That short fifty-mile span between Asia and Alaska with Big Diomede, Little Diomede and Fairway Rock lying like stepping stones between, impressed him, and except for one thousand miles, the Aleutians which almost touched Japan.

Later as a flyer in France in World War I, General Mitchell learned the advantage of an air force, and saw ahead to the day when armies, dreadnoughts and 'battle wagons' could be easy prey to 'those flimsy flying crates put together with a few bolts, glue and wire.'

After the war he continued to campaign for an increased air force for national defense—especially for Alaska, whose nearness to a potential enemy he knew so well. For these untiring efforts he faced court martial by the general staff of the Army and Navy and demotion to the rank of civilian. But the story did not end there. Billy Mitchell had been born too soon, that was all.

HOT HOUSE TOMATOES grown near Nome (Curtis & Miller photo).

Little and Big Diomede Islands, showing dividing line betwee America and Asia.

INTERNATIONAL DIVIDING LINE, Diomede Island—Big Diomede, Russian-owned, Little Diomede, U.S. owned, and Fairway Rock—lie midway between Alaska and Siberia. International boundary bisects 2½-mile span between. In summer Eskimos pile into oomiaks, set out gaily to visit friends and relatives on opposite shore with no regard for who owns what. Some load carving and handwork into kayaks to trade with tourists on steamers in Nome roadstead. Others land on sandy beaches to camp and dry fish; or in winter on land heads linked with solid, frozen highway (Nowell photo).

Lush Country but Lax Attitude

Gold seekers found the northland rich in so many ways. Almost overnight the tundra became a brilliant blending of fireweed, buttercups and forget-me-nots. Blueberries, cranberries, lingon berries and raspberries were theirs for the picking. Where nature had so lavishly bestowed flowers and berries surely gardens would also flourish. The U.S. Agricultural Department set up experimental stations to test the soil and experiment in growing fruits and vegetables for northern use. Where wild strawberries grew, tame berries with care should also grow.

But while Uncle Sam expanded his aid to Alaska in some departments, he curtailed others. Acres of forests were placed in reserve. Coal and oil lands were withdrawn from development and bird and fish and wild life preserves restricted hunting and fishing.

The country slid toward depression as development ceased. Wild protests bombarded Congress until finally a commission was sent to investigate. But without a voting representative in Congress, Alaskans were impotent.

SURVEYOR laying out Seimic shot lines, Kenai Peninsula (Brenneis photo).

Alaska in the New Century

Attraction of the Nome gold fields faded as the mining district fell into organized control of mining men and big machinery. While hundreds of gold seekers saw little but misery and hardship now in Alaska many felt a freedom in the northland and a peculiar bond with the land.

This Alaska, no longer unknown, presented a challenge to the trapper, the prospector and the 'just curious.' The wilderness, the rivers, presented endless opportunity and 'what else' for men weary of intrigue of a moneyed world.

Perhaps they could discover another Treadwell, or Kotzebue, or Anvil Creek, or a Ruby Beach. Already it seemed the great Oversoul of the North was weeding out the misfits, while the chosen ones were being assimilated into the fabric of the country. Eventually these would be a part of a civilization which was sure to come. A vigorous civilization it would be, for only the strong would survive.

Already sourdoughs self-assured were demanding some recognition by the United States, other than the appeasement offered in 1906—an offer of representation by a delegate to Congress, with influence but "Still No Vote," echoed thro the land. Prospectors fanned out over Alaska in greater numbers. One by one trading posts were established at the confluence of rivers and each man became a walking newspaper of the land through which he passed. A lonely life? Not to them, for theirs was a pioneer's vision. The love of a place untouched by civilization and somewhere a golden treasure which would startle the world. He's a strange breed of man, the true prospector, who finds contentment over an old pipe, in the patter of raindrops on a tent or the thunder of a cataract he had passed that day. There is the lonely wolf howling for its mate on the far hills where there should be gold, but wasn't.

This Alaska was really a paradise for sportsmen. Schools of salmon in the sea and trout in the mountain streams—moose, deer, caribou, mountain sheep and goats! Brown bear, black bear, white bear and Kodiak bear! A wild untamed region to hunt in and a rugged mountain region to get lost in!

FELIX PEDRO who discovered gold on Tanana River in 1902.

Then, GOLD! MORE GOLD! In Central Alaska! North of the Klondike. "Felix Pedro discovered gold on the Tanana, twelve miles from the Chena Slough. $40,000 washed out in one season (1902) on Pedro Creek."

Again bold headlines flashed across America. And a third stampede was on—pell mell for the Tanana Valley. Six hundred miles down the Yukon men came, following the ice jams. Then up the Tanana they went, poling their boats, scows and dories three hundred miles up-river.

Dawson's floating population came and the restless ones from Nome, still seeking. Little boats, big boats and sternwheel steamers, pushing ahead of them two and three and four barges loaded with stampede goods.

Felix Pedro, an Italian prospector from Oregon, first white man explorer in Tanana Valley, had struck it rich. In earlier days natives from the coast had brought blankets, beads, tobacco and Russian trade goods to barter with the Tanana Indians for furs. Later traders from Hudson's Bay Company and free traders intruded with better trade goods. Here also Fred Harper had established a trading post.

Now prospectors with pick, shovel and gold pan deluged a part of Alaska as yet unknown.

Ten miles down the slough from Chena a dozen large sternwheelers snubbed their bows to the bank of the Tanana River to unload cargoes of miscellaneous freight—groceries, merchandise of all kinds, mining machinery, household goods, barrels of whiskey and kegs of beer, perhaps a piano, and roulette wheels. Round about fluttered the dance hall girls. Everywhere disorder, excitement, hurry. This was embryo Fairbanks, its main street a muddy tundra road, flanked by saloons, tents, log cabins typical of a stampede town.

Chena rivaled Fairbanks for supremacy as a city but the shallow slough, unpalatable to steamers, decided her fate. Great deposits of gold were discovered, gold, tin and platinum. Immediately roads, and telephone lines fanned out to the creeks, reaching finally Valdez and the Copper River Valley. Railroads were extended to Iditarod, the Kuskaquiem, Koyukuk, Manly Hot Springs and the Copper River.

Far to the south capitalists added coal and minerals to Alaska's contribution of fish, fur and gold.

SENATOR FAIRBANKS and party in Alaska (Hegg photo, 1900).

U.S. Public Discovers Alaska

The United States found that this latest offspring was no longer a babe in cariboo parka but a lusty vigorous adolescent, howling for recognition, in a voice lawmakers could no longer ignore. In 1900 Senator Fairbanks paid a visit to the home of this lusty offspring, collecting data which would be of assistance in directing affairs until Alaska became of age. The party was awed, from the time they gazed at the grotesque faces on the totem poles to the time they viewed the glaciers.

The turn of the century (1900) also brought tourists, newspapermen and special interest groups. Seattle which had benefited so richly as a seaport town sent the Chamber of Commerce to make further survey. They too saw the forests of

totem poles and with no "aye, yes or no" appropriated one tall totem while the tribe was absent.

Old great-grandpa, too old to hunt and fish, had watched the theft of the long totem pole from the door of his shanty. Money, once so useless, to the natives had taken on value with their freedom. This time there would be no burning of villages. Chief Wm. K. Kininuock moved for an indictment and sent the City of Seattle a bill for $10,000 for one long totem. Seattle paid the bill and erected the totem pole in Pioneer Square, where to this day it looks down on a busy thoroughfare.

Time has made the totem pole symbolic of the Pacific Coast and a lucrative business for native wood carvers.

NATIVE WOMEN, Wrangell, 1900 (Hegg photo).

Summer Was Tourist Time

From Mexico to Maine they came, delighted with the curios and the stories which still breathed a musty aura of pioneer days. Fred Carolyn of Olympia, Washington was quite proud of the store he had opened in 1889 at Wrangell. On the counter lay a native straw hat, woven in native coulee style. The price? Fifty cents.

One day his friend, Mr. Wright, got off the steamer. In the short visit Mr. Wright shamed his friend to charge for an old greasy straw hat. Through several years the straw hat became the source of humorous arguments as the friends met.

"Perhaps we should raise the price to $5.00," suggested Mr. Carlyn one day, but no sale. Later the price was raised to $50.00 by adding another zero. Among the flock of enthusiastic tourists let loose one summer was a dowager from New York. With roving eyes she spied the straw hat and demanded to know its history.

"'Tis the hat of the great chief, Segalie Tyee; him that carved the first totem pole. Him that sent thunder and lightning," Mr. Carlyn explained. The lady examined the straw hat, smiling at its history. The boat whistled. Quick decision dropped fifty dollars on the counter. With the hat cuddled under her arm, she hurried away.

"Fifty dollars? You just never can tell about a tourist."

FAIRBANKS in 1904 (Curtis photo).

MALASPINA GLACIER. Alaskan sightseers wandered from alpine meadows to spectacular glaciers which crawled like gigantic sloths through age-old ravines. And they saw dead ones receding into the mountains which gave them birth (Hegg photo).

HEALEY'S STORE opened in Wrangell in 1878 with Red Cross sign in window. Town is home of totem pole and Indians still call place "home" (Robinson photo).

FROST IN MINING TUNNEL
(above center).

Benny's Flag

It happened in 1927. Governor Parks of Alaska remember that while all the states and territories of the U.S.A. had flags, Alaska had none of her very own. So with the help of various organizations he launched a flag design contest in the schools among the grades 7 through 12.

Benny Benson, a motherless 13-year-old lad in the Jesse Lee Home mission home at Seward was the winner. Benny explained, "I took a piece of art paper, 10 by 14 inches in size and colored it dark blue. Then I drew seven stars for the Big Dipper and the North Star. The blue is for Alaska's sky and the forget-me-not, Alaska's flower. The North Star is for Alaska and the dipper is for the Great Bear which means strength."

And Alaska exploded in delight at Benny's flag.

BENNY BENSON

PLACER MINING near Fairbanks (Above left and right) From muck and gravel, sometimes 200′ deep, embedded in earth mixed with bones of mastodon, long-haired buffalo and wild ox of past ages, miners extracted $75 million and end was not yet (University of Alaska).

APPEAL TO UNCLE SAM in *Klondike Nugget,* Dawson, 1902.

"When Do We Get Help?"

Just as the natives had found it difficult to forget the hard boot of Russian rule, Alaskans held a mistrust of the U.S. government which was so surely neglecting them now.

Time had separated the pioneers whose roots had sunk deep into Alaska's soil from the drifters with a 'get-rich-quick' philosophy. The pioneers worked for continued prosperity. For three decades they clamored for a larger measure of self-government and replacement of non-resident officials who like the 'carpet baggers' of the south, knew little of Alaska's needs and cared less.

Bills for statehood began drifting around Congress in 1906. With gold fever subsiding and mining governed by eastern capitalists, opposition to large interest began to grow until it became the vital political issue in elections. After a very bitter fight Congress signed Judge Wickersham's bill for Home Rule for Alaska on August 12, 1912.

SWANSON RIVER UNIT NO. 2—second producing gas
well on Kenai Peninsula (Wells photo).

Natural Gas
in
Alaska

FIRED NATURAL GAS from a Kenai field.

SEIMIC SHOT-HOLE drilling rig (above) on special tracked vehicle and fuel rig (Brenneis photo).

QUICK TRANSPORT of drilling tools to oil location (left). Oil was discovered in Alaska by Col. Edwin L. Drake in 1859 and on Kenai Peninsula in 1957 (Wells photo).

BURNING OF DUTCH HARBOR by Japanese (Photo Alaska Sportsman).

Comes the War

In December 1941 Japan bombed Pearl Harbor! In June 1942 Japanese carrier-borne aircraft bombed Dutch Harbor, Alaska, with some casualties but minor damage. A few days later Japanese troops landed on the Aleutians at Kiska and Attu. After capturing a lieutenant, ten men and a small naval detachment at Kiska, they were in full command of the island. Landing on Attu, not occupied by any American forces, they moved the entire Aleut population, and Mrs. Jones, the school teacher, to Hokkaido, Japan, leaving the island entirely to the Japanese garrison.

Japanese submarines now patrolled the Aleutian Islands and the North Pacific Coast. A troop transport carrying five hundred troops, tons of ammunition and T.N.T. was fired upon in the Gulf of Alaska, crippled, and was forced back to Seattle.

Now with the Japanese entrenched on American soil, the American high command prepared to take Kiska, Attu and the Aleutians. Woefully handicapped by a lack of information on the Aleutians, without maps of mountains, the army moved into some of the fiercest fighting of the war. But on May 30, 1943, the battle of Attu ended and the Aleutians were again American.

Though shrouded in censorship, the victory at Dutch Harbor was undoubtedly the turning point in the Pacific war. Had the Japanese chosen to invade rather than retreat, military authorities agreed, that from their foothold in Alaska, they could have bombed Kodiak and Anchorage and firmly entrenched they could have carried the war to Canada and the United States.

SALMON CATCH, Ketchikan (Roger Dudley photo).

Resources Unlimited . . . But—

While the petitions for statehood were ignored, they nevertheless left an impression on many lawmakers and made known the needs of Alaska.

Fur remained the basis for Alaska's economy. Fur trade opened up the valleys of the Yukon, Kuskaquiem and Tanana. Trading posts grew into potential cities. Gold discoveries drew men interested in mineral wealth which reached an all-time high in 1916 because of the Kennecott Copper mines—$48,632,138.

The salmon pack exceeded fifty million dollars and produced seven million cases in 1914-1918.

In 1930 Alaska was caught up in the international economic decline. But a depression could not starve Alaskans. There was game outside the door, berries on the hillside, fish in every stream, and lacking the ability to hunt, there was always the native, generous to a fault, with dried salmon and frozen cariboo.

So they held high their banner. They still had the land, sunsets, mountains and the northern lights. And neighbors with a warm hand clasp. And so in the lull, they planned for release from economic bondage which only statehood would give.

LATTER DAY SITKA.

U.S. AGRICULTURAL STATION

Anchorage—Boomtown

World War II boosted Alaska into the lime-light and the army boosted Anchorage into a boomtown, the center of military operations in Alaska, of communication, of transportation, of trade and culture. This city with no industry, no agriculture, no visible means of support is the fastest growing city in the United States. It is an air-minded city whose hopes for tomorrow rest on oil exploration and development.

The biggest construction year ever, 1959 changed the skyline with a sixteen-story hotel, Western Hotels chain, costing eight million dollars—Capt. Cook Hotel, ten million dollars—a Medical Dental building, $700,000—the Northern Lights Shopping District, $1,000,000—Inlet View Apartments, and a modern stable for forty horses —a new First National Bank with drive-in facilities—three new churches—a $300,000 telephone expansion—a new port, eight million dollars. These are but a few of the projects launched as Alaska enters statehood.

The Fur Rendezvous at Anchorage is a 'fun for all' time and a 'all for fun' time. The buyers come, mostly by air, from California, New York, London to bid for the most beautiful furs in the world, at the most famous auction in the world.

To this great annual celebration skiers fly over

the pole from Norway, Switzerland, and Sweden to compete with Alaskans. Top bands, actors, entertainers come from the United States. From all parts of Alaska come 'dog mushers—men and women and children—to compete in the Fur Rendezvous three-day, 75-mile dog derby championship race. Truck loads of snow are hauled in for dog sled events.

From the Diomede Islands and far north come Eskimos for the 'blanket toss' dance program and athletic contests, and each day is high-lighted by the outdoor fur auction held in front of the city hall.

There is a Queen of the Rendezvous, a coronation ball, a Miners' and Trappers' ball. There is square dancing, parades, and baby contests, modeling of next year's fur styles. No fur exchange fascinates buyers like the annual Fur Rendezvous of Anchorage. Since 1910 the Federal Treasury has gleaned 35 million dollars from fur sales whose only profit to Alaska previously had been wages paid to natives and processors of furs at Foulke Fur Company. In 1958 the government received five million dollars from Alaska furs.

Statehood will give Alaska seventy percent of the fur profit.

Sitka (Curtis photo).

SUMMIT LAKE on Alcan Highway, Mile 392 (Bilvic Studio photo).

Growing Season Short— But Sweet

The season for growing in Alaska is short— from 80 to 120 days; but research proved that long hours of summer sunlight coupled with the sub-irrigation given off by the thawing of frozen ground beneath, were a decided advantage.

Successfully adapted were potatoes, celery, lettuce, peas, beets, squash, carrots, turnips, cabbage and cauliflower and such small fruits as blueberries, currants, raspberries undercut the cost of imported foods. Forage crops—hay, alfalfa, and clover produced dairy feed and field peas ensilage. They found grass that matured late in the south would ripen along the Aleutian chain, and tests provided it high in protein value for cattle.

One million acres of land in various parts of Alaska were found suitable for farming, raising dairy cattle, meat, poultry, eggs, berries and grain. After years of propaganda, in 1915 Judge James Wickersham laid the cornerstone for a school of agriculture and mining at Fairbanks.

As time went on other courses were added and the name changed to 'The University of Alaska.'

Highway to the North

Included in 'Tony' Diamond's program for Alaskan defense in 1934 was the building of a highway across Canada linking Alaska with the United States. Not until the Japanese occupation of Alaska which menaced sea lanes was the highway considered necessary.

In 1942 the U.S. Army Engineers with the assistance of the Canadian Army Engineers, moved to construct a road from rail head in Canada to Fairbanks, Alaska—a road 900 miles from Seattle, Washington, to Dawson Creek, Canada, and 1500 miles more to Fairbanks.

The highway north to the forty-ninth state follows the Cariboo Highway, on through rugged mountains, over rivers and long stretches of wilderness, past trading posts and lonely cabins, to Dawson Creek. Then comes the long span to Whitehorse on the Yukon. It's a long road, but trucks such as the Lynden Transfer trucks cover 2500 miles in four days. Tons of freight roll over the road, the perishables protected against heat and cold. And they call it the Alcan road.

The U.S. Army has played a most important part in the development of Alaska, constructing railroads and highways, building sea walls (as in Nome) and generally lending their expert knowledge wherever needed.

UNIVERSITY OF ALASKA in 1950. Institution had its beginning in 1915 when Judge James Wickersham, Alaska pioneer, laid cornerstone on July 4, naming it "The Agricultural College and School of Mines."

Airfields Developed

After the attack on Dutch Harbor by Japan in 1942, airways were intensified. Military requests were approved in 1943 when the six major airports were increased to 806, adequate for war needs.

Planes sent by the United States to the western front and Russia ferried up over Canada, over the air routes established by the C.A.A. to air bases in Alaska, then they were flown over Siberia to confront Hitler's Luftwaffe. Thus Alaska's airways became crucial in the two-front compaign which finally overcame Hitler and his Nazi army.

Militarily, Alaska became the guardian of the north, and North America. Eskimos have made excellent adjustment to the white man's branch of civilization, showing amazing ingenuity in mechanical repair work. Because of this infinite skill they are in great demand in the far north air bases where white men must adjust to climate and living conditions.

The Military Front

World War II alerted military authorities to the need of fortifying Alaska. In 1940 work began on two major bases near Anchorage, Fort Richardson and Elmendorf Air Field, and Ladd Field, a 'cold weather' testing station near Fairbanks. Realization had come that Alaska was the jumping-off place for lend-lease material—tanks and aircraft—for the U.S. allies and Russia.

A cutback in military spending followed the war. Only the peace hoped for did not return. Another ogre raised it head—Communism. Alaska began to assume even greater strategic importance in a free world with the realization it straddled the route to Asia and the army began to spend millions of dollars in Alaska and because of that development cities are growing, the population is increasing and settlers are arriving seeking new opportunities.

ADAK AIRFIELD, Mt. Moffat in background (Robinson photo).

FORT RICHARDSON, Anchorage (Robinson photo).　　　　　ANCHORAGE, 1957 (Robinson photo).

Dew Line Established

Where once revenue cutters were the sole protection of the bleak Aleutian Islands, where in World War II the Japanese landed, today's Dew Line reaches invisible antennae in a widening search for enemy approach. Built at a cost of twenty-five million dollars by Manson-Asberg Company of Seattle for the U.S. Air Force, the Alaska District Corps of Engineers project stands as a first line of defense.

The building of these northern defense bases was no sinecure. Starting from scratch on barren volcanic islands, the work included contractors' camps, with housing and mess halls. Fruit, meat and dairy products, all the soldiers' personal needs must be flown in from Seattle and Anchorage.

Flown in was material for construction of A.C.S. wave guide supports, reflector antennae and feed horns, huge radome bubbles—water, sewer and electrical systems—roads and runways for planes which furnish the only transportation to the mainland. Weather hampered them and fogs so thick they could not be scattered by 100-mile-per-hour gales. Not the least of the nuisances were the bears which converged on the mess halls.

U.S. REVENUE CUTTER *PERRY* (Gabbett photo).

MANTANUSKA VALLEY, Garden Spot of Alaska (Curtis & Miller photo).

VEGETABLES GROW FAST
and big in Mantanuska Valley
(Robinson photo).

Alaska's Garden Spot

During the lean years of 1935, poverty-stricken farmers of the United States seeking a new homeland chose the Matanuska Valley, Alaska, as the place of migration. Experimental work had already demonstrated the agricultural possibilities of this area. Two hundred men with a thousand dependents from Michigan, Wisconsin, and Minnesota set out on the long trek to build new homes.

These first homesteaders, built log cabins, cleared land, planted crops, raised chickens and cattle, each year experimenting with different seeds and new crops. Cattle increased, homes grew more comfortable, the barns more modern. Today Matanuska Valley supplies the north with a great percentage of meat, fresh vegetables and dairy products.

The Agricultural Experiment Stations at the University of Alaska at Fairbanks, Petersburg and Matanuska continue to seek new crops and new animal types, suitable for the north. Palmer, nearby the main trading town, fulfills the needs of a farming community with modern schools, churches and a hospital.

ALASKA RAILROAD circling Mt. McKinley (Curtis photo).

Railroad Aided Alaska's Growth

In 1914 Congress approved railroad construction linking Fairbanks with the coast, and the initial growth of Alaska was begun. In 1947 the road was modernized. Steel and concrete replaced wooden bridges and 115-pound steel rails replaced the 70-pound rails. In 1950 a modern depot was built.

A special type of engineering and know-how is required to build a railroad over frozen northern terrain. There are many hazards in sub-arctic train operation, not the least of which are the moose herds which browse on the tundra.

The Alaska railroad, winding through the most scenic country in the world, takes one to the front door of McKinley National Park, within walking distance of a modern hotel and Alaska's wonderland.

REMAINS of dead glacier (Hegg photo).

167

MUSK OXEN imported for Eskimos (Warwick photo U.S. Fish and Wildlife).

Wildlife Haven

Alaska is a land of surprises. One came when in 1898 a dredge or pick bit into the frozen carcass of a prehistoric animal. Entire bodies in perfect preservation were excavated.

Often ivory tusks, sometimes six feet long, blocked the work, deep in the mining shaft. The U.S. Fish and Wildlife found this discovery of special interest. Here was an idea for another source of food and wool. If these huge mammals could thrive in the long ago years, why not transplant the buffalo and musk ox?

Alaska was a land of varied topography and climate. From the rain forests on the coast to the tundras of the north, and from the treeless plateaus of the interior to the alpine meadows tucked high in the mountains, a variety of pasture made a paradise for the wildlife suited to that area.

In 1928 the Fish and Wildlife Service moved twenty-three bison from the National Bison Range in Montana to the big Delta region of Alaska, where it was found they survived the cold winters. Today the herd numbers several hundred. Later a small herd of musk ox were imported, a source of wool and food for the Eskimos in time of need.

PREHISTORIC MAMMALS (photo American Museum, New York).

Appealing for Statehood

Alaskans have cooperated with remarkable solidarity for statehood. The final struggle for statehood was fought since 1945 under the leadership of E. L. Bartlett, the last of Alaska's delegates to Congress. "We need statehood desperately. We need two U.S. senators, a representative, and state government with power to act. We are entitled to all the rights of American citizens."

Prior to Mr. Bartlett, 'Tony' Diamond, deceased in 1953, fought for statehood. During an incumbency of ten years he kept insisting, "with statehood Alaska will no longer be a beggar at the national table, but be a recognized member of the household, eligible for all benefits and responsibilities."

Next to statehood Mr. Bartlett begged for defense as had General "Billy" Mitchell before him. "Establish bases at Anchorage, Fairbanks and the Aleutians—I say to you, Defend the United States by defending Alaska. Is it not obvious that an enemy moving across the Pacific must first invade Alaska?"

But his bill asking for ten million dollars for air bases failed to pass. Then in 1939 came World War II and suddenly the need for air defense became all important.

E. L. BARTLETT, last delegate to Congress.

NATIVES TANNING MOOSE-HIDE for clothing and shoes.

PACIFIC NORTHERN AIRPORT, Anchorage (Robinson photo).

From Bush Pilot to Airline

Bush pilots began to change transportation in Alaska after World War I. Pioneer flying rescue work, delivery of food, material and men to places inaccessible by other means of travel colored the life of the early pilots and the manner and means by which they eventually built airlines is a story all its own. A few died in bed but more died in accidents. Many failed to succeed and many fell by the wayside.

All the Alaska airlines today are managed by these bush pilots, grown up. Noel Wien of Wien-Alaska Airlines started as a bush pilot in 1925. Ray Peterson of Northern Consolidated Air Lines and 'Mud Hole' Smith of Cordova Airlines were flying in their areas in the early thirties. Bob Reeve of Reeve Aleutian Airways had an operation out of Valdez in 1934. Bob Ellis, president of Ellis Air Lines, flew as a navigator for Ancel Eckman in 1929 and made the first non-stop flight from Seattle to Juneau, April 15, 1929. He is still flying in Alaska.

Alaskans like to fly. They fly everywhere. Kodiak with a population of twenty-five hundred flew 18,182 passengers in a year's time. Anchorage, the largest city in Alaska, has two airports with a combined total of landings and take-offs greater than any American city with the exception of New York and Chicago.

Nine commercial air carriers including three foreign lines—France, K.L.M., and Scandinavian Air Lines systems—use the facilities of the international airport. Few passengers are Americans. The majority are business and professional men coming from New Guinea, Europe, Denmark, etc. to the United States.

Today Alaska is less than a day from any point in the United States. Ketchikan is but two hours and forty minutes from Seattle, via daily flights.

Thus air services draw Alaska closer to all of us; her problems have become our problems, her welfare our concern.

Prospectors today are a different breed of men than the old time prospector. Schooled in universities, a graduate from the school of mining, he has no degree in the School of Hard Knocks. The appeal of mountain streams, and clean solitudes is lost to him, except as the possible location for a mineral deposit. Time perhaps will build up a yearning for wilderness places, but his equipment includes geiger counters, scientific gadgets —and vitamins.

Since there are few cow pastures in which to land, flying in Alaska is more hazardous than elsewhere, but the flying prospector of today is as much at home in his plane as the native was in his kayak.

170

FLIGHT OVER ICE AND ROCK (Robinson photo).

Will Airplanes Replace Dogs?

Dog teams, the mainstay of early transportation are still necessary however, where delivery must be made to inaccessible places. Early bush pilots considered dog teams and their masters as guardians of the great land of ice and snow. Many a flier owes his life to a dog musher who crawled over ice fields and foundered to his rescue in some forbidding spot.

Perhaps 'whirly birds' will replace the dog team. Over one hundred helicopters already meet real needs, for they require no airport, since they get down and off the ground in any open space. Already they have carried freight, steel, lumber, cement; they have rescued people, dead and injured, dropped hay to starving horses and wild life, lifted up power line poles and set them in their holes. They are cheaper and quicker than a pack horse, and haul more than a dog team.

But the old prospector, what became of him? Still in a class by himself, he follows the yearnings of his heart, searching for a new land as much as gold, a faithful dog his only companion.

PLANE LEAVING FOR INTERIOR (Ellis Air Lines photo).

"TOMORROW WE'LL FLY"

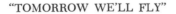

171

AT STEPEN LAKE HUNTING CAMPS (Vogel photo).

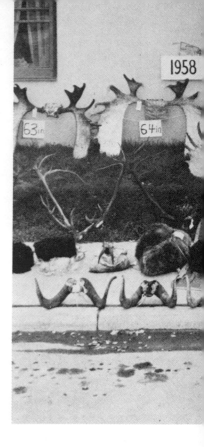

Big Game Hunters' Paradise

A hunting trip in the Far North is a never-forgotten event in any man's life. Kodiak bear, cariboo, Dall sheep, mountain goats . . . giant moose roaming Alpine meadows . . . Grizzlies cuffing salmon from the lakes and rivers at spawning time . . . King salmon, steelhead, and dolly varden . . . this is Alaska. In the fall the wilderness is filled with an awesome beauty. Vibrant reds and yellows flame like torches against the green forest or live again in the placid waters of a lake.

Alaska today has hunting services in every lo-cality sponsored by experienced guides and outfitters. For safety reasons, no man hunts on his own. Typical of such service is that provided by O. H. Vogel, outfitter at Anchorage: "Stepan Lake Hunting Camp—Fog Lake Camp—one of seven—location Talkeetna Mountains—altitude 2600 feet—11 lakes in timberline country—amphibian and pontoon lake service—good camps—experienced guide for each hunter—excellent trophies."

NATIVES OF NULATTO, as well as Aleuts, Eskimos and Indians, owe allegiance to U.S. They are still the best hunters and trappers, and thru education at Bureau of Indian Affairs, schools or State Schools, they hold key positions in transportation and industry. They serve efficiently in state legislature and in government offices, are unsurprised as instructors in fishing, mining, carving (Curtis 1900).

INDIANS HEWING CANOES

ALEUTIAN (above), Alaska Steamship Co., bound for North (Wood photo); below, loading
S.S. *Nadina* (Alaska Steamship photo).

CHENA LEAVES SEATTLE for Alaska (Alaska Steamship photo).

New Day for Steamships

Since the time of Alaska's purchase in 1867, for less than the value of one shipload of salmon, over sixty steamboat companies had entered and left the trade. The Alaska Steamship Company, entering the trade in 1895, has weathered the economic storms and played an important part in the continued economic development of Alaska.

Whether carrying freight and passengers to canneries and villages in out-of-the-way places or cities, whether unloading at a dock or dumping freight and passengers to a raft or rowboat, Alaska Steamship has a record of reliability and consideration for its clientele.

Gold rush times never lacked a passenger list going and coming, but shipping was a one-way haul since the time of copper ore. Today five times as much cargo goes north as comes south, for Alaska still imports over 90 percent of all requirements. New industry could change this.

Improved methods of handling cargo are easing the economic pressure. Shipping in containers loaded and unloaded by derrick onto ships and railway cars for interior Alaska cuts the costs. Already the 13-ship fleet of the Alaska Steamship Company has undergone this change for the new day just dawning.

WRANGELL in 1908 (Case-Dudley photo).

VALDEZ in 1910 (Curtis photo).

The Stikine River Country

Wrangell, the third oldest city in Alaska, was established in 1834 by Admiral Baron Wrangell. It was here that Russia established herself to keep the Hudson's Bay Company from encroaching in her fur-gathering territory. Historic with totem poles and steeped in Indian lore, it is truly an interesting, picturesque city.

Through the years salmon and shrimp fishing have been its main support. Once fruitful in furs, Wrangell now turns its attention to timber and as the forests to the south recede, Alaska timber reserves take on importance.

The Wrangell Lumber Co., one of the largest mills in Alaska, and the only one exporting, is affiliated with the Alaska Lumber & Pulp Co. of Tokyo, Japan, which processes annually some 15,000,000 feet of lumber.

The area is rich in minerals, gold, silver, and marble. It is a paradise for fishermen and hunters, and can be reached by air, by boat, by car and ferry in summer, via British Columbia.

Economy Built on Fish

Gateway to the interior, Valdez is located on the rugged coastline of William Sound. Its growth began in the gold rush days of 1898 as a tent city when it was the port of entry for men and supplies. Today this mild-weathered picturesque city can be reached by the Richardson Highway. With boat service to Seattle and bus service to the interior, it is a tourist's paradise.

Valdez has given Alaska two champions for freedom, first, 'Tony' Diamond, once mayor of Valdez for nine years, and a member of the Territorial Legislature for four terms, who voiced the slogan, "Alaska would not progress unless it had statehood." Second, Valdez was hometown to Gov. William Egan, the first elected governor of Alaska.

CORDOVA in 1910 (Robinson photo).

Cordova's Future Bright

Mountains of almost pure copper drew the Guggenheim interests to Alaska at the turn of the century. A railroad was built up the Copper River and Cordova was born. From these mountains came the copper which Baranov used to give the church bells fashioned in Sitka, their special tone. Cordova prospered during the years when copper ore came by train, 195 miles inland to the coast, for shipment to the smelters at Tacoma, Washington.

Then in 1938 the mines played out and the rosy future of Cordova faded for a time. The railroad was dismantled, its only reminder a history as told by Rex Beach in 'The Iron Trail.'

Cordovians returned to fishing, prizing the salmon run up the Copper River. In the years of a big run they closed shop and everyone went fishing. The future is bright as the U.S. Forest Service makes its surveys of timber, coal and oil. The prospect is good that tomorrow will bring back the days of copper, with pulp mills and oil refineries.

The Ketchikan spruce lumber mills which operate eleven months of the year, in 1952 had a

SEWARD—ice free port at head of Resurrection Bay. Cradled in lap of mountains it is surrounded by bold, rugged beauty. Big game and big fish make it hunters' paradise and resort area. In 1915 Pres. Wilson selected busy seaport as terminus for rail route to Fairbanks, extending some 412 miles north, branch lines touching various mining districts (Robinson photo).

KODIAK. Where raising of sheep and cattle failed in Russian regime, 5,000 animals are now being grazed by 50 operators on 1,654,259 acres under leases granted by Bureau of Land Management. Some 22 million acres suitable for grazing could support 200,000 animals. Most grazing is carried on in south central parts of Kodiak Island where Japanese current tempers mild winters, offers longer growing seasons. (Norman Photo Shop).

KETCHIKAN SPRUCE MILLS, Tongass National Forest.

capacity of 100 B.M. per eight-hour shift. The modern equipment included an eight-foot band mill, a six-foot re-saw, 10 × 60 edger, 40-foot automatic trimmer. The company operated its own dry kilns and logged a portion of its own requirements.

In 1957 the pulp mill at Ketchikan was enlarged to produce up to 480 tons per day of high quality pulp. As yet there are no furniture factories in the district, as the high freight cost to the United States market makes the price prohibitive. At present there is an embargo on logs which protects the natural resources from rapid depletion, and encourages the manufacture of forest products in Alaska.

Tongass spruce is as majestic as the Redwoods of California. It is estimated the Tongass National Forests and the Chugac National Forest on Williams Sound contain 85 billion board feet of timber.

Alaska still imports 100,000,000 board feet of lumber a year for its construction. It is hoped this can be remedied by the mills now being constructed for production in 1960 at Sitka, at a cost of $55,000,000 by the Alaska Lumber & Pulp Co. The year-round employment for hundreds of workers will give impetus to Sitka's economy.

CRUISING TIMBER in Tongass National Forest (Shipp photo, U.S. Forest Service).

FALLING GIANT SPRUCE, Tongass National Forest (Thackery photo U.S. Forest Service).

WILLIAM A. EGAN

William A. Egan became the first governor of Alaska in November, 1958, with a vote surpassing that in any previous election in the history of Alaska. Taking the reins of government in strong, sure hands he launched an active development program that led to a 65% increase in the gross volume of business during the first years of statehood.

The land is no longer virgin, populated by hostile tribes of natives. Fortunes were dug from the frozen ground far greater than Solomon ever dreamed of. And more remained to be dug.

The natives now face a new world as do all of Alaska's citizens. All of them are working together to bind the mountains, lakes and rivers with the tundras and flower-draped valleys . . . to turn this potential wealth into a more livable, more prosperous land.

The Sphinx of Ophir, looking out over the wide tundras of the Seward Peninsula, was to speak out at last:

"I hear the tread of pioneers,
Of millions yet to be;
The first low wash of waves where soon
Shall roll a human sea.
The elements of Empire here
Are plastic yet and warm
The chaos of a mighty world
Is rounding into form."

WHITTIER

181

Index